Our Universal
Spirit Journey

Our Universal
Spirit Journey

*Reflection and Verse
for Creation's Sake*

by

John P. Cock

tranſcribe books

Dedicated to
my two sons

John and Jeremiah

colleagues on the journey

Other books by John P. Cock

Motivation for the Great Work:
Forty Meaty Meditations for the Secular-Religious (2000)
with foreword by Thomas Berry

Called To Be:
A Spirit Odyssey (2nd ed., 2000)
how a mountain boy becomes a citizen of the universe

The Transparent Event:
Post-modern Christ Images (2nd ed., 2001)
a book about the meaning of life

See Web bookstores or e-mail
tranScribe-books@triad.rr.com
or go to Web page
www.johnpcock.homestead.com

Acknowledgments

Besides spirit guides now, throughout my life, and throughout history, I thank the following who helped me with this book: wife Lynda and son John, who sense after our readers, and son Jeremiah for his technical support; colleague Ellen Howie for her art that graces the section pages; friend Alex McKeithen for his design and art for the cover; colleague Randy Williams for his reflections along the way; and I thank Thomas Berry for his friendship and the inspiration of his prophetic vision.

Mandalic Sketches by Ellen Howie, Altamont, NY

Wheel of Time, p. 34
Sacred Moment, p. 92
Labyrinth, p. 162

Foreword ~*Thomas Berry, April 2002*

Throughout the universe, spirit is the all-pervasive presence, sustaining and guiding the diverse components of the universe as they fulfill their manifold destiny. As spirit is one, so the universe, in its primordial origin, its movement through time, and its final fulfillment, is a single, if infinitely diverse, mode of being. This book is a simple, direct, and exuberant statement of the all-pervasive presence and power of spirit.

As the author's thinking is dominated by this awareness of spirit, in his writings he seeks to awaken others to a similar awareness. His life dedication is to assist in bringing a healing remedy to the contemporary disturbances in the human community and in the life systems of the planet. Our need for such interior guiding and healing becomes ever more urgent as a new age of anxiety takes possession of the human community in these opening years of the 21st century.

Our present difficulty in managing the human project and its relation with the Earth project is seen as rooted in eliminating spirit from our understanding both of ourselves and the world we live in. Our inability to appreciate this pervasive spirit dimension of the natural world he sees as leading to the difficulties we are now having in our relations with each other and with the planet itself.

He also sees spirit as a transparent reality throughout the universe. Developing a continuing consciousness of such presence both in individuals and throughout the society must be the central work of anyone who would guide us through the disturbed events of the present. To achieve this consciousness we need only realize that we are heirs not only to the deeper teaching of our western religions but also to the teachings of the other religious-spiritual traditions of the world.

The historical realism of western traditions, whatever

their benefit, might be considered as the most obvious difficulty we experience in accepting this emphasis on spirit in its unity and its universality. Yet we do have the guidance of persons such as Hildegard of Bingen in the 12th century, of Francis of Assisi in the 13th century, and so on into the later centuries until our own times when we see the spirit powers of Gandhi and Schweitzer and so many others.

While there are extensive efforts at renewal within our contemporary western world, we begin to realize that the difficulties we are experiencing will never be remedied from within the context in which they arise. Indeed the difficulty of economics is not in economics, it is in the psychic realm of excessive desire for wealth and power; the difficulty of government is not in government, it is in the lack of inner human and spiritual bonds within the community. So with the various phases of life in our times. The difficulty is in our dysfunctional interior life. None of the external adjustments will provide exactly what is needed. The attack on the Towers was not an assault on innocence but a response to the arrogance expressed in the architecture and in the exploitation of the entire world emanating from the Towers.

John Cock's account of his own experience through these last four decades provides a background for the ideas that he is presenting. He has lived with people in different parts of the world, for example, in India and Indonesia. From these experiences he has gained perspectives that are deeper and more encompassing than if he had only the insights available to us in America. Thus, his is not so much an explanation of "how" but more a narrative of the realities of our historical existence along with a wide-embracing listing of contexts in which spirit becomes manifest in the course of human affairs and the universe journey.

What is here is a firm commitment to the reality of spirit, the unlimited diversity of its modes of functioning, and its ever-present support for the Earth Venture and the Human Venture as together we journey into the oncoming centuries.

Contents

Section Three: **Spirituality in the Ecozoic Era**

Spirit is always aready present . . .

<u>Verse 1</u>

let me put it simply
     Spirit is the key to life

all of Earth's beings know
     Spirit is the key to life

all her religions know
     Spirit is the key to life

Jesus and Buddha knew
     Spirit is the key to life

Spirit awakens us

Spirit reunites us

our *raison d'être*

—*may 2002*

A New Context

SITTING IN THE LAUNDROMAT about three weeks after the events of September 11, 2001, major wake-up calls of my lifetime passed by in review:

- World War II and Hiroshima
- Assassinations 1948-1981
- Earthrise 1969
- Terrorist Attacks 9/11/2001

I was almost three that December 7, 1941, when Japan attacked Pearl Harbor. Watching the movie *Pearl Harbor* this past summer reawakened those childhood recollections of war. Mama was so sad because Daddy was called up, then ecstatic when he didn't have to go. I was anxious overhearing the adults talking about our dropping atomic bombs on Hiroshima and Nagasaki, August 6 and 9, 1945.[1] Then I was agog watching the adult neighbors run out of their houses right through our ballgame, hugging and whooping, "The war is over! The war is over!" But the image of the mushroom cloud seared my consciousness from then on. When we visited Japan and Hiroshima in 1970, the unbelievable consequences of those first nuclear attacks really woke me up.

On January 30, 1948, at about age nine, I became aware of Gandhi's assassination at a theater newsreel showing the funeral procession through the streets of New Delhi. The little man who freed India was killed by a fanatical Hindu's bullet at point-blank range because "Gandhi is a Muslim-lover." His legacy of nonviolence came home to me years later as I lived and worked in

17

villages of India, and in particular, the one where his Sevagram Ashram was located.

In my early twenties, I was shaken by the assassination of UN Secretary-General Dag Hammarskjöld. On his way to negotiate a cease-fire in the Congo, September 18, 1961, he went to his death in a fatal plane accident that many think was sabotage.

Next came the rifle shot(s) that killed my President, John Fitzgerald Kennedy, November 22, 1963, as I studied in the university library. My life direction radically changed as I told the chairman of the department that the Ph.D. program didn't make sense to me any more, that something had to change in our society, and that my research project on Robert Browning wouldn't make much difference.

February 21, 1965, Malcolm X was shot and killed in Harlem's Audubon Ballroom, a year after becoming an orthodox Muslim after making the hajj. His assassins were vaguely identified as Black Muslims. On April 4, 1968, Martin Luther King, Jr., was shot down in Memphis. Two months later, June 5, 1968, Robert Francis Kennedy was slain in Los Angeles as he campaigned to become my President. And on October 6, 1981, Anwar al-Sadat, President of Egypt, took an assassin's bullet in the neck, quite possibly at the command of Dr. Ayman al-Zawahiri, a surgeon, now the chief lieutenant of Osama bin Laden — that is, if either is yet alive.

The assassinations of all these most revered, and hated, world leaders woke me up and deeply addressed my life.

As a result, by early 1969, my wife, young son, and I found ourselves working and living in a ghetto on the West Side of Chicago, trying to make a difference in civil rights. On July 16 of that year, I sat with the rest of the world watching the Earthrise on TV. The phrase "indivisible, with liberty and justice for all" took on new meaning. I became a citizen of the Earth that day. Seeing the Earthrise woke me up.

Now I've lived long enough to see two planes crash into the twin towers of the World Trade Center and another into the Pentagon. At this point, no images will outlast those. I am awakening again to a new world and wondering about its meaning.

How do we talk about the meaning of existence? Old belief systems set in old worldviews do not work. Consider as evidence the global argument about "God's will" and which nation or religion is truly "His chosen" one.

After September 11, I became aware in a new way that the three religions of Abraham — Judaism, Christianity, and Islam — often seem to be talking about three different gods rather than the one God of Abraham. What has become painfully clear is that our beliefs and language cause division and even war. It is absurd that over half of the population of the world who started out with the same God of Abraham are so prone to warring — especially in the Middle East, the West, and Central Asia. If our symbols and language divide us, then let's do something to change that, for if dialogue is blocked, communion is blocked. We have to do better for the sake of the future of humanity and the whole Earth enterprise.

To do something about the symbol system that divides us on the planet, we can begin with our most common symbol, "Spirit." Spirit reality is our most objective reality — strange as that sounds to a culture dedicated to a scientific worldview — for what is more real to all humans than the experiences throughout each day of our lives, waking up each morning reflecting on new possibilities and going to sleep each night in reverie. Life experience and how we reflect upon it is Spirit's medium. We need believable and profound metaphors to reflect upon our experiences. And now, more than ever, we need a common way to communicate the profound meaning of life. I cannot think of a better word symbol than "Spirit" — though it too has its problems.

We will talk about "before" and "after" the attacks on New York and Washington from now on because we have been forced to rethink our planetary relationships. I hope September 11 will prove to have been a transforming spirit event for our planet, enabling us to make a destinal leap forward.

Reflections from a small group I attended afterwards are most telling: "9/11 was a kaleidoscope for me — all the pieces are the same but all are shifted. . . . I was changed from a national to an earthling. . . . For some strange reason, the people of the world are more like brothers and sisters to me than ever before." Spirit is leading us beyond our divisive ideologies, is leading us to rediscover our oneness. Unless this happens we will continue to mutually dis-create rather than mutually recreate the Earth and everything on it.

> The task before us now, if we would not perish, is to shake
> off our ancient prejudices and to build the earth.[2]
> **~Pierre Teilhard de Chardin**

Teilhard says also "we can progress only by uniting." These times and Teilhard's imperatives to unite and build the Earth are revealing to us the depth and power of Spirit; are compelling us to live as one community; are redefining spirituality for the 21st century; are calling forth new spirit people and leaders. A fresh wind is blowing. I have to believe something new is emerging.

> *Leader*: These are the times.
> *People*: We are the people.[3]
> *All*: Creation is blest.

jpc
Greensboro, North Carolina
May 2002

Spirit is the key to life . . .

Prologue:
Where I'm Coming From

Spirit is the inner dimension of everything,
        the dynamic of communion within creation.
It gives foundation to but transcends religions
        and cultures.
Spirit is ever sustaining the immense journey
        and making all things new.

Spirit is "always already" present.
Creation is transparent to Spirit.
All are on Spirit's journey; therefore, all are spiritual.
Spirit sustains, awakens, forms, engages, unites.
Since all religions are Spirit literate, "Spirit" is
        our most universal holy word.
Human-centeredness contradicts a recreated Earth.
Human development is becoming creation-centered.

The spirit revolution of our time abounds.
We can stand on the sideline, deny it, resist it,
        or respond to Its call that eternally sounds.

I WAS RAISED A PROTESTANT CHRISTIAN in the West, and in the Bible Belt of southeastern USA. From that, one can make many assumptions about my religious upbringing: that it was

    Bible-centered
    conservative to fundamentalist
    under a cloud of sin
    personal-salvation oriented

otherworldly
pious and self-righteous
focused on beliefs based on rather nonsensical creeds
racially bigoted and economically classist
human-centered, believing "man" is the center of creation
intolerant of other religions, even other denominations
patriarchal
gender-biased
ecclesiastical
and more American than Christian

I had much baggage to throw overboard as I journeyed. At the same time, I have kept much baggage by choice, for my religion

is based on depth spirit dialogue
is grounded in creation that is very good
is grace-centered
assures me that I am unconditionally accepted
is authenticated in vocational call and response
radically cares about the neighbor
will not tolerate idolatrous, self-serving faith
declares the meaning of life is to give it
trusts death-resurrection as the essence of the way life is

Not only have I been throwing out the excess baggage of my religion that does not make sense and that degrades existence; I have also been cherishing my religion's life-giving foundation. Some would call me a "heretic": I go along with the definition of that word that says I pick and choose those parts of the tradition that make sense and put the other parts away in my "agnostic box" to look at another day. How can anyone believe what s/he cannot believe?

*****

As a young family, my wife, Lynda, and I took our two sons and lived all over the world for most of two decades, in U.S.

ghettos and third world villages in Indonesia and India. Our greatest learning came as we lived and worked with the poor and people of many faiths: Muslims, Hindu, Aborigines in Australia, Jews, Parsi, Buddhists, Anglo- and African-American Christians, and secularists.

The family order style of common life was the main vehicle for our journey. Many of the families who performed the work of the Ecumenical Institute: Chicago/Institute of Cultural Affairs[1] called themselves the Order: Ecumenical, or simply the Order. Day in and day out, we worshipped, studied, worked, and served together, always experimenting with new methods that we shared with communities, religious and secular organizations, and responsive people in general.

During those years in the Order, we corporately read and studied together tens of spirit writers. I came to appreciate deeply Joseph Mathews, Bultmann, Tillich, Bonhoeffer, H. R. Niebuhr, Kierkegaard, Buber, Gogarten, Kazantzakis, Merton, Otto, Ignatius of Loyola, John of the Cross, Teresa of Avila, Teilhard de Chardin, Gandhi, J. S. Dunne, Camus, E. E. Cummings, Lao-Tzu, Ortega y Gasset, Eiseley, D. H. Lawrence, Kuhn, Susanne Langer, Hesse, Frankl, Eliade, Simone de Beauvoir, Husserl, Castaneda, Boulding, Tagore, Segundo, Joseph Campbell, Huston Smith, Malichi Martin, Ken Wilber, and many others.

Our quality of life in the Order was never to be equaled. After returning "home" to recuperate and make money to help put our sons through college, I was in the "desert" for about seven years before my passion oozed again as I began to teach and write. I first wrote with pain and doubt about the needed reformation in the church, emphasizing underlying contradictions and strategies. Next, I relived my life through writing my memoir, *Called To Be: A Spirit Journey*, rediscovering my resurgent spirit journey. I reunited with my old spirit guides listed above and judged that the deep dialogue with them and my Order colleagues had not been enough communicated.

Imaginal education, formulated by the Order and the Institutes out of Kenneth Boulding's *The Image*, says that real learning takes place when an alternative image intrudes into one's consciousness and calls upon an existing image to defend itself in the debate for truth. For example, we went further than anyone I know in transparentizing Christianity (Section II), which means that one can see the essence of life through any encounter in creation. Part of what triggered my decision to write my second book, *The Transparent Event: Post-modern Christ Images*, was my reading several of the Jesus Seminar books by Funk, Crossan, Borg, Geering, and Wink, and attending a conference at Duke University, "Jesus in Context," with Crossan, Borg, Sanders, Wright, Fredricksen, and other New Testament scholars. They all helped occasion a truth debate within me.

*****

Huston Smith, one of the guides listed above, describes the four stages of human life according to Hinduism. My wife and I discovered we have followed that tradition well in the third stage, *retirement*, which is anytime after the birth of the first grandchild: pick up stakes and move, lest "associates would treat you as they always had"; become forest dwellers; work out your philosophy of life, lest "life ends before you understand it."[2] After the birth of Kaitlyn, we moved to a wooded area in Greensboro, North Carolina, where we began to consider our philosophy of life and new directions.

For many reasons we have been lucky to end up in Greensboro. One of the best reasons besides being close to our sons and grandchildren has been becoming friends with Thomas Berry. He describes himself as a geologian. His greatest passion is articulating the story of the universe, a big enough context for the great work of all humans of whatever persuasion. Fellowship with him and studying his latest book, *The Great Work: Our Way Into the Future* (along with *The Universe Story, The Dream of the Earth,* and several other books) inspired my third book, *Motivation for the Great Work*: *Forty Meaty Meditations for the Secular-Religious.*

Thomas Berry's concept of *intercommunion* throughout his works does not stop with what we normally think of as ecological. His context includes the cosmology of religion, or the spirit *milieu* of creation. We are very clear that deep spirit encounters call us to and sustain us in the great work.

During the last few years — and the last few months when all globally have observed the divisiveness of religions more than usual — I have begun to see that maybe it is not enough to reform our major religions, though that task must go on. Yet, the reform task must not overshadow the primary strategy needed for our time: rediscovering our one, universal Spirit tradition. We must go far beyond the ecumenical and interfaith activities of the past. We must claim our common spirit journey for the sake of our common Earth future.

*****

Throughout human history we have been inventing words to address *That* which encounters us, and especially in the West since the Enlightenment. Sure, new words feel funny, and even phony, during experimentation. I thought a lot about which words to use in this book. At one time I was going with "holy spirit," no caps. I even considered "psychic-spiritual" dynamic. But I have settled on "Spirit," with a capital "S," not to designate a deity, creator, or designer, but to point to the most important word about the most important dynamic in existence.

Sometimes new language gets us into trouble, especially with fundamentalists, who are sure holy writ was foreordained from the beginning of time and is never to be changed one iota. But invent and reinvent we must, for the future of the planet depends on our being sure we are all in tune with the same reality rather than playing the dangerous game of my divine reality is better than yours. Deep global unity will not come until we are convinced we are all talking about the one, same reality in life that sustains, motivates, and unites us.

Because all religious traditions are "Spirit" literate and use "spirit" language, why not start with this common word to describe the universal dynamics of our experiences? It makes sense to me that the word "Spirit" is more universally used than the word "God" and is therefore the best word for our common, ultimate reality. Since language is an invention, why can't we intentionally use a word symbol that communicates with the six billion human citizens of Earth? Unifying symbols have everything to do with our future together on the planet.

Whatever resonates deepest and truest while always maximizing the human dialogue is what I'm seeking to articulate as we consider together our one, universal spirit tradition. Let us honor all traditions by honoring Spirit, the dynamism of what was, is, and will be, even as ancient Hinduism intuited:

> Then even nothingness was not, nor existence.
>   There was no air then, nor the heavens beyond it.
> Who covered it? Where was it? In whose keeping?
>   Was there then cosmic water, in depths unfathomed? . . .
>
> But, after all, who knows, and who can say
>   whence it all came, and how creation happened?
> The gods themselves are later than creation,
>   so who knows truly whence it has arisen? . . .[3]
>
> ~*Rig Veda*, X:129

All we know for sure is that creation has arisen and keeps arising, which leads me to believe Spirit preceded God-talk.[4]

Also, the word "Spirit" is harder to make into a graven image. It's less of a person and more of an energy, force, and power. And in the understanding of the Christian trinity, "Spirit" is no less than "God" or "Christ." For those who still prefer God and Christ language, they can be assured that the Judaic-Christian Bible is full of the "Spirit of God" and the "Spirit of Christ" phrases, so I trust they can hear the word "Spirit" with those ears; and that Muslims can hear the word "Spirit" as the "Spirit of Allah" from the Koran. Among the rest, Eastern and other nontheist religions are becoming a large percentage of our human population.

No definition of the word "spiritual," even in the unabridged dictionary, satisfies me. That's another reason I'm writing this book: the definitions are either ethereal or religious. What I'm trying to do is to rearticulate the depth dimension of reality in the universe and in existence.

I ask you the reader to keep in mind that we are attempting to reinvent the word "Spirit" in order to overcome our "flatland" perception of life that is killing our spirit. Losing the depth dimension of life is the same as losing the spirit dimension. Nikos Kazantzakis, therefore, cajoles us:

> Battle with myths, with comparisons, with allegories, with rare and common words, with exclamations and rhymes, to embody[5] . . . to make the Spirit visible, to give it a face . . . that it may not escape us.[6]

We are about making Spirit visible again, transforming flatland by reintroducing the depth dimension of life. As we reconsider the deepest mysteries of life, we invent the words that freight their meaning. Meaningful interpretation of universe truth and experience can help us swim the river of radical consciousness and not drown, especially during chaotic times like these.

The bottom-line is this: Spirit is more important than the air we breathe and the food we eat. Maybe we will understand as our ancestors before us did that we are seeing the depth dimension of life, its tragedy, its awesomeness, its interconnectedness, its blessing. And like our ancestors, may we see that life is good because Spirit is at its heart.

*****

Of course, I write from the human perspective, yet in recent years I have become quite conscious of our being human-centered in the way we look at life. Said positively, my operating context is shifting from human-centered to creation-centered, which I experience as a mighty struggle.

Spirituality has to do with "transparency," our seeing through creation and life-events to the meaning of reality. Therefore, all creation in all its forms and through all of its sensors is transparent to Spirit — Spirit can reveal Itself through anything, anywhere, anytime, through a stream or even through you and me.

> Like the little stream
> Making its way
> Through the mossy crevices
> I, too, quietly
> Turn clear and transparent.[7]
> **~Ryokan**

Is nature Spirit? Of course not, but it is transparent to Spirit. Am I Spirit? Of course not. No thing is Spirit, but everything is potentially transparent to It. And no one or no religion has the market on Spirit — It's Its own thing. It's wild yet on creation's side, from my experience of It. Spirit is gracious and awesome. Since Spirit is the most real thing there is, everything depends on It for its vitality.

The search for some perfect spiritual state that will produce some sort of pure action is *not* what I primarily mean by spirituality. The fruit of authentic spirituality for me is taking our human wisdom and technologies, that we have been using badly as far as the biosphere — including humanity — is concerned, and transforming their use for the good of the whole Earth community.

Maybe the Spirit of the universe is revealing to us that we are stuck — evolutionarily speaking — in our human-centeredness, which is devolving the Earth community and holding it back. Spirit is about getting us unstuck. Spirituality is about saying *Yes* to Spirit's urging toward unity.

*****

This is where I'm coming from and where I stand, having taken a long Spirit-led journey that has moved me from my Protestant Christian beginnings, to seeking that tradition's reform, to trying to help articulate Spirit's depth and how It works in our lives making them meaningful. As I have let go of the literalism of my religious and cultural tradition and have embraced truths of other and emerging traditions, pain and joy have attended my way. I have been crossing over for some time and now find myself dedicated to a universal dialogue with Spirit.

Profound unity, in the midst of the profound divisiveness of our time, is riding on the subject of this dialogue. Spirit is that dynamic in life that unites. If there are few signs of unity, it's because we are out of touch with Spirit. The more unity we experience and see manifest in creation and its societies, the more we live in touch with Spirit that is recreating our vision for the Earth and tailoring our commission of service.

If that be so, we have the foundation for the comm-unity of all beings and can see what St. Francis saw: that animal, vegetable, mineral; time, space, matter, energy; events, relationships, and experiences — that *all* are kin. In his hymn *All Creatures of Our God and King*, we meet "brother sun," "sister moon," "brother wind, air, clouds, and rain," "sister water," "brother fire," "dear mother earth," "thou, our sister, gentle death," not to mention our billions of human sisters and brothers, including the past and coming generations of all species. We are all on the immense journey together, guided by Spirit.

I truly believe Spirit is the key to life, not economics, politics, education, nor religion. This is where I'm coming from.

Verse 2

My Tradition's Spirit Words

Whither shall I go from Spirit — It is always here

Spirit was, is, and ever shall be

Spirit loves the world and gives Itself to and for the world

all are sons and daughters of Spirit: the stars, mountains, and creatures

everyone who believes in and acts out of Spirit has abundant life

the wind of Spirit blows where It will

Spirit is reconciling the world

Spirit dwells among us, full of glory

Spirit is making all things new, rough places plain, and the crooked ways straight

Spirit is like a refiner's fire

Spirit is the way, the truth, and the life

no one comes to fulfillment except by Spirit

Spirit is all about sacrificial love

Spirit is resurrection power

Spirit is always coming again

Spirit never leaves us comfortless

where two or three are gathered in Its name, Spirit is there

great things will the children of Spirit do

Spirit is the be-all
                    and end-all

—january 2001

"Wheel of Time" by Ellen Howie

Section One

Our Universal Spirit Journey

THERE ARE AT LEAST TEN REVOLUTIONS of our time that are making a big difference, positively or not. In this section we will consider one of those, "The Spirit Revolution," and later, in Section III, "The Cosmological Revolution." Both are revolutions in human consciousness. We will make reference to the other revolutions throughout the book, for how can we consider the spirit journey in any other context than what's going on in our times?

1. The Spiritual Revolution
2. The Cosmological Revolution
3. The Global Revolution
4. The Ecological Revolution
5. The Democracy Revolution
6. The Urban Revolution
7. The Women's Revolution
8. The Nonviolence Revolution
9. The Transnationals Revolution
10. The Techno-Scientific Revolution

The revolutions of our time are changing us as human beings, and consequently changing creation. We humans have genetically modified crops and food, have taken charge of the Genome Project; we are cloning animals and are about to clone humans; we have modified the weather — wittingly and unwittingly — and have drastically diminished the natural resource base of the planet.

35

("Resources" is a good example of our human-centered worldview: we think natural resources are for us humans to *use*.) We humans have definitely revolutionized the way our planet and atmosphere work, or do not work as well as they used to before the human onslaught, from about 10,000 years ago till now.

The appropriate question is What is the emerging context for all the revolutions? The question is no longer What is best for the human? The futuric answer can no longer be a human-centered response.

At the beginning of the last century we still believed in "progress," by which we meant human progress at any cost. Now, over a century later, more and more are convinced that human progress has hit the wall: human progress in science, technology, economy, governance, peacemaking, education, and quality care has proved itself to all humans as grossly inadequate as we look at the state of our planetary community. How do we rebalance the imbalances we have let loose in everything from terrorism, to greenhouse gases, to diminishing species, to increased warring, to billions of economically and spiritually impoverished human beings?

The question in which we humans play a destinal role is What is best for creation? "Human development" is no longer the big context for the journey we're on. Therefore, as the name of this section states, we are all on the universal spirit journey, the journey to the heart of being, and back. How then do we begin to talk about our one spirit journey in these revolutionary times?

Verse 3
Till All Breath is Gone

We got Enlightened
descended Mt. Myth
to the Promised (flat) Land
where there was fact and
human progress instead
of milk and honey.

Thousands, hundreds of years
to climb the mountain
only tens to come down
for decline is faster
than ascent; throwing
out stories faster

Than creating great myths.
who's to say which is
better: mountain, flatland?
both are illusion —
the one otherworldly
the other immortal
empiricism.

Whether heavenly or
this-worldly progress
we are left in limbo
for our lives are about
seeing through to the meaning of birth and breath

Not chasing promises
that someday will come
in the sweet-by-and-by
or at retirement —
given new gold watches
to wind going home.

So promise us some height
some depth and substance
right now, downtown Flatland.
we know we're not
el cap'tans of our fate
so let's deeply breathe.

Let us have a go at
our interiors —
everlovin' moments
experiencing
wonder and fulfillment
till all breath is gone.

—august 2001

Reflection 1

The Spiritual Revolution: Making All Things New

> [Ours is a time of] mixing, a stirring together of the "essence" of religion, namely, spirituality. . . . The Dalai Lama has observed that "the reality is that the majority of people today are unpersuaded of the need for religion." He calls, however, for a "spiritual revolution."[1]
>
> **~Matthew Fox**

> A world empire without emperor can happen only when universal order and meaning is mediated through all native soils and symbols but contained by none.[2]
>
> **~Lonnie Kliever**

> Save the Planet
> All Is One
> Love All, Serve All
>
> **~*Hard Rock Café* t-shirt** (Myrtle Beach)

I CAN'T THINK OF A MORE SECULAR INSTITUTION than a *Hard Rock Café,* and I can't think of more profound spiritual messages than the ones on their t-shirt. (Yet, I would rearrange their order: "All Is One" first, as *the* spiritual reality of creation; "Love All, Serve All" second, as universal spiritual wisdom; and "Save the Planet" third, as our spiritual manifesto for the community demanding our allegiance.) These three secular messages are indicative of the widespread consciousness of Spirit in our time.

My drafts of this reflection before September 11 had an introduction here that was out to convince you the readers that we are in a time of spiritual revolution. Hopefully, the events of 9/11 have convinced us all that the revolution is at hand. I cannot imagine a louder wake-up call. It was an assault upon our global way of life that operates out of nationalism, religious and racial divisiveness, economic inequity, military supremacy, women's subservience, and a general disregard of the natural world.

September 11, 2001, confronted our way of knowing, doing, and being. We will have to make new decisions. We will have to relate to "what is" differently, because what is, is not what we thought it was. A new set of relations, a new ethics, and a new set of priorities for a new global agenda are demanded. A new way of life has to begin. That is not to say we will not try to continue to live out of our old ways. We will. But we can't. We must reinvent what it means to be human to continue living in our planetary community. Time was split so deeply that day that we cannot cross the chasm and go back to where we were. Impossible. Illusory. But we will try.

Something new has begun to emerge. Our deep human responses in the aftermath of 9/11 have been about unity, care, love, heroism, respect, altruism. Our spirits were opened. We cried, consoled, reunited, and reflected on another level. We realized our lives are not mostly about work and money, but about our relationships of value, quality, depth, and meaning on a local and planetary scale.

Because of the way life is, interconnected and interdependent, the 9/11 event has brought many closer to reality. We are longing for and sensing the reality of unity. We see the possibility to react with compassion and peace instead of vengeance and war. I maintain that this growing awareness is our response to Spirit.

Our encounter with Spirit also brings deep questioning. In humanity's past, religions grew out of the response to big questions about the origin and destiny of existence. Many expressions emerged, but one thing was at the heart of all religious expression: *Spirit is key.* We no longer live in a religious world or culture, despite all the howls to the contrary. Certainly, religions exist, and just as certainly bad religion exists and results in heinous crime. Jonathan Swift wrote, "We have enough religion to make us hate, but not enough to make us love one another." Even though religions exist, we are a secular world — but with a plus: a consciousness of and sensitivity to Spirit.

Spiritual questions now seem more piercing than ever before. Why? and What for? are certainly back. Why are we conscious? What is the purpose of life? If we are one planetary body, why are we destroying it? Why are we rethinking our fundamental relationships, even our religions? Why do we sense our interior reflection is at least as real as exterior fact? How do we talk about what we are experiencing when psychological language can't say it? What is ultimate truth in the midst of what's happening? What will bring us together and keep us together? Why is there such a longing for unity?

These are definitely spiritual questions. Their theme points to the mysterious wholeness and goodness of existence, even if we don't have explicit answers to what it's all about.

Spirit encounters us and births our acute consciousness. When something radical, total, and unconditional is demanded of us, we are experiencing Spirit. When something announces to us that we can go on, in spite of, we are experiencing Spirit. When something releases us to be slave to no thing and free for all, we are experiencing Spirit. When we see and respond to creation's suffering, we are experiencing Spirit.

Spirit is in our midst and is transforming us. We humans have come a long way in our relatively short history — about 2.6 million years since the first humans were standing on two legs and making tools out of rocks as one of the new species on the block — but we have a long way to go, and the whole way is a spirit journey.

"The Times They Are A-Changin'" is a truism, more now than when Dylan wrote the song. One of the biggest changes is in our spirituality. Following are signs of that change, leading me to believe that we are living in a spiritual revolution:

1. **More spiritual and less religious**. "The percentage of Americans who say they feel the need in their lives to experience spiritual growth has surged twenty-four points in just four years — from 58% in 1994 to 82% in 1998."[3] Obviously, there is more interest in spiritual growth these days. Physicians say spirituality aids the healing process. Studies and practitioners say that spiritual practices lower stress. People say spirituality adds meaning to their lives. Some even say that since the boomers have hit the age of fifty, many have become seekers. Another survey points out that 70 percent of Americans say we can be spiritual without going to religious services. We observe that during past decades Americans have become more spiritual in their assumptions and practices and at the same time less religious.

2. **The move from East-West dialogue to the global establishment of major religions**. Toynbee said the meeting of Christianity and Buddhism would be the most significant event in the history of our time. Buddhist gurus, seminars, meditation centers, religious orders, and publishing houses dot the West. One thing for sure, the major religions are in my country. The largest non-Christian organized religions in the U.S. are as follows: 5.6 million Jews; 4.1 million Muslims; 2.4 million Buddhists; 1 million Hindus.[4]

3. **Regular meetings of the Parliament of the World's Religions**. In 1993, they closed registration early with 9,000 participants and held their closing event at Grant Park, Chicago, with 75,000 in attendance. Their document *Towards a Global Ethic* is the first consensus by the world's religions on basic standards of ethical behavior. During its 1999 meeting at Cape Town, the 7,000 participants of the Parliament continued their inter-faith/inter-

cultural dialogue as well as spotlighting three-hundred service projects being done around the world. The 2004 meeting will focus on the next generation.

4. **The defection from traditional Christianity during the 20th century in European, Australian, and now American mainline churches**. In the USA there has been a surge in Baha'i, Muslim, Jewish, Buddhist, and Mormon communities in the last twenty years; a decline in the membership of Episcopalian, Lutheran, Methodist, and other mainline Protestant groups; and a corresponding slowdown in new church development among Roman Catholics and Eastern Orthodox.[5] One sociologist estimates that two-thirds of all boomers in the U.S. reared in organized religion dropped out, while less than half have returned.[6] At the same time, a poll provides evidence of a major shift in core beliefs among Christian communities of faith in the USA. For example, only about 20 percent of mainline church members affirm that one gets to heaven through good works. Only about 30 percent agreed with the statement that Christ was without sin, "an epochal change in popular theology" that suggests the growing loss of faith in the divinity of Jesus.[7] However, these shifts do not necessarily indicate that the rising number of "church alumni" is less spiritual. Many would even say they defected for spiritual reasons. Traditional religions, on the other hand, are growing in Russia and China.

5. **A swelling of the ranks of the Pentecostal and fundamentalist Christian churches**. Harvey Cox writes in *Fire from Heaven: The Rise of Pentecostal Spirituality and the Reshaping of Religion in the Twenty-first Century*:

> Rarely in history have so many models of reality and so many metaphors of what human life is intended to be, made their cases with such vigor and in such jarring proximity to each other. . . . To some it seems that today our shrunken world is heading for spiritual chaos, but others hope that out of the churning a new and unifying style of sanctity and a fresh planetary awareness may well appear.[8]

Cox adds "experience" to the list of authorities for religion, the other three being scripture, reason, and tradition. It can be said that "experience" is the/a hallmark of the Spirit revolution we are now in.

6. **A conservative trend in established Christianity in the West**. Some say the Roman Catholics, the Greek Orthodox, and the Southern Baptists will be the last religious institutions of the West to allow women authentic leadership roles, which would of course mean ordination. Observers judge the conservatism of Christian church leadership to be doctrinal, literalistic, moralistic, patriarchal, exclusive, and afterlife-oriented. Among conservative Protestants in the USA, powerful leaders such as Pat Robertson and Jerry Falwell have given motivation to the so-called Religious Right, the Moral Majority, and the Christian Coalition. One can also list as conservative, in a different kind of way, the Mormon Church, one of the fastest growing Christian communities. Some predict they will be second only to Roman Catholicism in size in a couple of decades. Another sign of conservatism is the Roman Catholic Church's fight against birth control at all costs, but in October 2001, the government of Guatemala, Latin America's country with the highest birth rate, overrode the Church — a radical departure — with a reproductive health policy of contraception and education. Will the closed systems of Christianity open or die? (The Roman Catholic Church is still getting rid of many of their best: Luther then, Matthew Fox now.)

7. **The Liberation Theology movement** began in Latin American in the early 1970s. Leonardo Boff and Gustavo Gutiérrez, among the founders of the liberation theology of "praxis" over "orthodoxy," preached and wrote that the Gospel is more about the style of sacrificial discipleship than belief in traditional doctrines. Some accuse them and their followers of political and economic agendas. They have answered by saying that the rich and powerful — mostly Christians in Latin America, for example — have oppressed the masses by structuring and perpetuating poverty. Many bishops, clergy, and laity have been martyred in the name of their faith. This movement has spread globally on behalf of the disenfranchised.

8. **Books on religion and spirituality lead sales growth in all categories**. According to the Book Industry Study Group, "sales of Bibles and prayer books, inspirational volumes, and books about philosophy and Eastern religions are growing faster than any other category, with the market expanding from $1.69 billion to about $2.24 billion in the past five years."[9]

9. **The New Age movement**. One thinks of healing therapies, tarot cards, witchcraft, holistic health, angelolatry, new age music, crystals, channeling, runes, UFOs, alchemy, paganism, astrology, theosophy, the occult, est, plus much, much more, when giving examples of the New Age movement. The long list is a sign that the rush for spiritual discovery in all directions is as real a phenomenon as established religious practices. The change that has occurred in America is well articulated by Elizabeth Lesser in her recent book, *The New American Spirituality*: the spirit path is that which each individual creates or discovers, not one given by some religious institution or authority. She uses the word "democratization" of the spiritual search as characteristic of the new spirituality of our time.

10. **The Jesus Seminar impact on the West**, including the writings of Spong, Borg, Crossan, Funk, and Wink, especially through mainline media (*Time, Newsweek,* major newspapers, *PBS* and major television channels), has promoted widely the new research and thinking about the historical Jesus, with all its revolutionary implications. Such scholars basically deny Jesus' divinity; say that Jesus did not say about 80 percent of the red lettered words attributed to him in the New Testament; and make Jesus out to be a spiritual sage. One knows their message is getting out, for traditionalists and fundamentalists have launched media promotions and protests to counter the Jesus Seminar.

11. **A returning to the founders of religions**. Besides the Jesus Seminar, Don Cupitt, a founder of the Sea of Faith group begun in Great Britain, focuses on the kingdom religion of Jesus in his book *Reforming Christianity*. He says in summary: the kingdom religion of Jesus is a message about love of life as given; about a sacrificial life-style on behalf of this world; about committing oneself to life and one's neighbor here and now without delay and therefore verges

on nihilism. This message and way of Jesus is almost humanistic (no metaphysical belief system or catechism), almost nonreligious (unstructured, of the heart, immediate, and intuitive) — in all, close to opposite of the church that has evolved, mediating salvation through its institutions, its texts, and its creeds. How do we get beyond the detours since Jesus and get back to his religion without beliefs: one that honors universals and not the tribe; one that is democratic, nondiscriminatory, and not the plaything of a religious establishment or ecclesiastical institution; one that is about the love of life more than the fear of death and questions about the afterlife; one that is committed to this moment and this world, knowing these are the gracious gifts of creation?[10] Another return to the founder that caused a stir this year is the biography entitled *Buddha,* by Karen Armstrong.

12. **The EarthSpirit movement**, catalyzed by the writing and speaking of Thomas Berry and his students Brian Swimme, Miriam MacGillis, Mary Evelyn Tucker, and others. This movement is dedicated to enhancing mutuality among the human and nonhuman elements of creation. They say the depth contradiction of the planet is our human superiority complex, fostered by religion and culture. They say the Earth, not the human, is the measure of all things on Earth, and that the universe is the only self-referent reality, meaning it is the measure of all things in the universe. Berry articulates well the foundation for this loose movement:

> The spiritual formation of humans in the third millennium will undoubtedly include . . . an immersion into the deep creative powers of the universe . . . [as] the most direct contact a human can have of the divine.[11]

Mary Evelyn Tucker writes of the approaches of various religions toward nature in four arenas:

Western and South Asian traditions
   seeing nature as metaphor: a stepping-stone to the divine
   seeing nature as mirror: a reflection of the divine

> *East Asian and indigenous traditions*
>   seeing nature as matrix: a meeting place for the divine
>   seeing nature as maternal: a nurturing presence for the divine[12]

13. **The new story of the universe**, as told by Thomas Berry and Brian Swimme in *The Universe Story,* is a new story of creation, its journey and transformation. This new spirit story of our time, like all our other spirit stories that have even birthed religions, came out of creation itself. Berry and Swimme's epic story goes to great lengths to scientifically articulate the thirteen to fifteen billion-year-journey of the universe. A story often creates the event that can transform and build a new culture. In this newest phase of the spiritual revolution, their story of wonder and union is over against an old dark story of sin and separation. We now know there is no absolutely true story about our journey, our culture, or our religion. All cosmic stories are myth built on fact. The cosmic story that makes sense is the one that's life-giving. Robert Theobald wrote in an e-mail entitled "Turbulence," just before his death in 1999:

    [T]he fourth story [after the hunter-gatherer, agricultural, and industrial stories] requires us to abandon beliefs that we have been developing throughout human history. We shall have to abandon our conviction that we can successfully dominant nature or other human beings. We shall have to accept that we cannot afford to exclude any group . . . without highly destructive consequences.

    The old stories of creation do not make sense to us now and are being abandoned, thus adding to the spiritual revolution. There is only one world. Spirit is in it or nowhere. This is a radically new understanding that has been simmering since Einstein, at least.

14. **God is panentheistic, not transcendent**, according to Matthew Fox, who has catalyzed a movement under the banner of *creation spirituality*, with an emphasis on original blessing rather than original sin. By "pan-**en**-theism" Fox means that Spirit is in everything and everything is in Spirit. Living out of this understanding, he says, one sees all creation as good and worthy of

care. Fox traces this understanding to Christian mystics such as Meister Eckhart, c. 1260-1327. The Roman Catholic Church did not appreciate Eckhart then nor Fox now. They silenced Fox and he has became an Episcopal priest.

15. **Realignment after the old split between matter and spirit**. Science and religion are seeing spirit as a dimension of existence, not a dimension beyond existence. Dannah Zohar/Ian Marshall's books are an example: *The Quantum Self, The Quantum Society,* and *SQ: Connecting with our Spiritual Intelligence.* Starting from the theory of quantum physics, they bring forward the thesis that there is IQ, EQ (emotional intelligence), and SQ (spiritual intelligence), this last being the faculty developed over millions of years that is prior to and integrates all human intelligences. Therefore, SQ is our ultimate intelligence. Ursala Goodenough, a leading America cell biologist, has written *The Sacred Depths of Nature*, a book about manifest spirit in biological life evolution. She ends each section of biological insight with overt spiritual reflections. The split is gone for her. And the split has gone for the likes of Ian Barbour and Holmes Rolston III, who have spent their careers reweaving the strands of science and religion. Rolston says, "Our creeds, like our sciences, are ever reforming."[13] Pierre Teilhard de Chardin is the most famous of those in this category. This priest and scientist said it well: "the world has a heart" and it is Spirit. His use of the word "noosphere," the envelope of consciousness ("superconsciousness") around the Earth,[14] is now being taken quite seriously by the Global Consciousness Project at Princeton that scientifically tracks and measures this envelope of consciousness from some thirty-eight locations around the globe. The worldwide web has many sites that keep up with the edge dialogue between science and religion: www.metanexus.net is one of the better ones.[15] Quantum computing is another example of what we are talking about here.[16]

16. **Spirituality in the workplace** is catalyzed by the notion that if we spend most of our time at work, why not make it as meaningful as possible. Deep thinking in this movement has come from Willis Harman, Joe Jaworski, Margaret Wheatley, Danah Zohar, Peter Senge, Peter Block, Peter B. Vaill, V. S. Mahesh, Juanita Brown,

David Isaacs, Parker Palmer, Alan Briskin, Russ Moxley, Tom Chappel, Ian Mitroff, Elizabeth Denton, Dick Richards, David Whyte, the Institute of Cultural Affairs, and many more. Also, Matthew Fox's *The Reinvention of Work* gives insight to the spirit depths of work. *Fortune Magazine* has done a feature article on spirituality in the workplace:

> The spiritual revival in the workplace reflects, in part, a broader religious reawakening in America. . . . People . . . refuse to bow to the all too common notion that much of the work done in corporate America must be routine, dull, and meaningless; they want and expect more. . . . Now more and more people are willing to talk about bringing faith to work. . . . They are choosing their words carefully. To avoid tripping over dogma, they speak of 'spirituality' and 'meaning,' not of religion and God. . . . [They are asking] the fundamental questions.[17]

As this trend accelerates, all sorts of new partners coalesce. The Spirit in Business: Ethics, Mindfulness and the Bottom Line conference scheduled in New York during April 2002, was "a world conference of business leaders, decision-makers, and change agents." Finally, go to Barnes and Noble (bn.com) and browse the many pages of books on "leadership and spirit" addressed to the workplace.

17. This is part of a larger **spiritual potential movement in the West** that is pushing spirituality in the workplace, sex, business, politics, art, sports, childrearing, etc. People are beginning to see their lives as integrally whole, or the traditional separation between the spiritual/secular is blurring. Champions of this movement are Michael Murphy and his integral transformative practice, Ken Wilber, who has initiated the Integral Institute, and Andrew Cohen, who believes along with Wilber that enlightenment cannot be attained nor achieved, only that Spirit can be discerned and confessed as present here and now.

18. **Neurotheology**. "Religion and the Brain," *Newsweek,* summarizes recent findings of psychologists and neurologists as they seek to pinpoint which regions of the brain turn on and off during spiritual practices such as meditation, prayer, and ritual.

Gallup polls in the 1990s found that 53 percent of American adults said they had had "a moment of sudden religious awakening or insight." . . . By pinpointing the brain areas involved in spiritual experiences and tracing how such experiences arise, the scientists hope to learn whether anyone can have such experiences, and why spiritual experiences have the qualities they do. . . . The bottom line . . . is that "there is no way to determine whether the neurological changes associated with spiritual experience mean that the brain is causing those experiences . . . or is instead perceiving a spiritual reality" [Andrew Newberg, University of Pennsylvania]. . . . Since "we all have the brain circuits that mediate spiritual experiences, probably most people have the capacity for having such experiences," says [David] Wulff [Wheaton College, Massachusetts]. . . . In a nutshell . . . they use the data to identify what seems to be the brain's spirituality circuit.[18]

What is different in these studies is that the researches are taking spirituality more seriously than in studies in earlier decades. MIT Press recently published James Austin's 844-page study on the subject. Such studies are becoming established in the scientific-academic community.

19. **The awesome spiritual questions raised by the times** are calling forth reflection among all peoples, especially questions of meaning, value, purpose, and justice: we can go to the moon and live in space, so why can't we wipe out terrorism or poverty? If we can stop HIV/AIDS, why don't we? If we can stop drugs, why don't we? If we can stop destroying the planet and atmosphere, why don't we? If we can save species from extinction, why don't we? If we can stop military escalation, why don't we?[19] Such questions have never been as realistic as they are now, and therefore never so personally and collectively addressing. Duane Elgin articulates it this way:

What we're really facing is the convergence of a number of powerful trends — climate change, species extinction, the spread of poverty, and the growth of population [now add terrorism after 9/11]. All of these factors could develop individually, but what's unique about our time is that the world has become a closed system. There's no place to escape, and all of these

> powerful forces are beginning to impinge upon one another
> and reinforce one another. . . . It's going to be another couple
> of decades until we reach the breaking point.[20]

Bill Moyers' documentary on PBS, *Earth on Edge*, June 2001, highlights natural Earth crisis after crisis in numbing repetition. Watching it, I experienced a similar mood in myself as in the 50s when nuclear holocaust seemed possible. Revolutionary changes happen in the midst of such crises when penultimate challenges of survival and quality of life are raised.

20. **Many have helped catalyze the spiritual revolution of our time**: **Gandhi and the nonviolent movement**, including Rosa Parks and Martin Luther King, Jr., of the USA, Lech Walensa of Poland, Vaclav Havel of the former Czech Republic, Tiananmen Square demonstrators of China, Nelson Mandela and Archbishop Desmond Tutu of South Africa, and John Hume and David Trimble of Northern Ireland, demonstrating that individual/social acts change history dramatically, not some otherworldly force; **theologians** such as Buber, Tillich, Bonhoeffer, Teilhard de Chardin, and Wiesel, who revolutionized western Christianity and Judaism by insisting that Spirit is the primal dimension and dynamism of creation; and those **spirit-motivated persons** of our time who have understood that a sacrificial mode of existence changes creation, such as Mother Teresa, Dag Hammarskjöld, the Dalai Lama, Victor Frankl, Archbishop Romero, Thomas Merton, Thomas Berry, and others mentioned above. The new spirit persons and movements are becoming more secular, strategic, social, and intentional, addressing issues related to healing the Earth and reconciling human divisions caused by war, terrorism, poverty, and injustice. Such persons have made deep decisions that have enhanced traditional images of what it means to be human. Many contend that their life-styles came as a result of what can be generally called spirit encounters.

THESE ARE A FEW OF THE MANY SIGNS, mostly from a western perspective, that begin to point out the newly perceived power of Spirit amongst us. I have tried not to make judgments as to the individual merits of the twenty signs, yet I do believe that many of these directions can lift us above divisive religious doctrine, literalism, otherworldliness, and moralism. Together these signs portend a universal spiritual revolution.

The revolution caused by Spirit in our time would cut out any religious middleman and call for a planetary priesthood of all beings, who are aware of their experience of the spirit dimension of reality and are responding to spirit eventfulness with a *Yes* decision, not out of a set of beliefs or a set tradition.

Planetary spirit consciousness is emerging at accelerating speed. No longer need we settle for the old "flatland," materialistic, humanistic, or even religious truths. We are awed by what's happening as we yearn for and experience unity. We know that the lasting solutions to the contradictions of our time will be born of our sensitivity to Spirit. We know we are primordially bound to all that is, and, therefore, our new story has to be universally inclusive. We know that there is only one world and that Spirit empowers it, seemingly more than ever before.

Again, the holistic and revolutionary edge of what's said here is on that secular *Hard Rock Café* t-shirt that captures spirit reality ("All is One"), universal spiritual wisdom ("Love All, Serve All"), and the spiritual manifesto of our times ("Save the Planet" in its human and nonhuman manifestations). The consciousness of Spirit working in universal existence is emerging whether we consider ourselves religious or secular.

Parker Palmer, an educator cited above, in these excerpted lines from his poem "Grand Canyon,"[21] witnesses to how Spirit encounters him during his life journey:

> And Spirit cuts like water through it all
> Carving out this emptiness
> So inner eye can see
> The soaring height of canyon walls within
> Walls whose very color, texture, form

Redeem in beauty all my life has been
The darkness and the light, the false, the true
While deep below the living waters run
Cutting deeper through my parts
To resurrect my gravebound heart

Making, always making, all things new

I too believe Spirit is *always making all things new*, especially in times like these.

'Tis

Ancient: all is in Spir-iT
Buddhism: consciousness of Spir-iT
Sufism: children of Spir-iT
Christianity: transparency to Spir-iT
Taoism: manifestation of Spir-iT
Judaism: awesomeness of Spir-iT
Hinduism: oneness with Spir-iT
Islam: allegiance to Spir-iT

all my religions tell me
who I am

Spir-iT creature

we are
Spir-iT creatures
created by iT
transparent to iT
reflecting iT
creating with iT

seamlessly
at one
with iT
eternally
graciously
and
anxiously

so let us be
who we are

thankfully
embracing
embodying
announcing
the fact
of our lives

Spir-iT is

'Tis

—january 2001

56

Reflection 2

Our One Spirit Tradition:
Spirit-Talk for Creation's Sake

all my religions tell me
who I am

Spir-iT creature

we are
Spir-iT creatures
created by iT
transparent to iT
reflecting iT
creating with iT

~jpc, from ""'Tis"

I AM NOT A CHRISTIAN FIRST OF ALL, not even a human
first of all. I am a member of creation, having journeyed here
from the beginning, rising out of the dust of planet Earth. I am a
member of this universe, about fourteen billion years old am I. As
a DNA code-carrying member, I am a part of all that ever was and
ever will be in this universe.

How did all this happen? I was born into it. Sprung up
from it. I meditate on how sad I would have been if I had not
made it, if one of the untold number of sperm had not connected
at my conception. I just showed up miraculously and am inheritor

of all that has ever been. I am not, as Joseph Mathews used to say, a "tweeu": *those who eternally envy us* because they didn't make it.

I made it! We made it: the girl I married made it; our grandchildren made it; Haji Mabub, the religious leader of the cluster of villages where we lived outside Jakarta, made it; that squirrel on our lawn outside our window made it; the rocks beside our door made it; the creek down in the woods made it. We are all lucky duckies according to Dr. Seuss.

I am one of the lucky ones who made it into creation. This is the most profound image I have of who I am, one who has been created and is being created — one who knows all this to be an absolute fact. Anything less than the fullness of this image is a reduction of who I am, and not really true.

This image stated, I can begin to talk about the other particularities of who I am. I was born in the 20th century, Caucasian, male, part of the Cock family, in a small town in Virginia — part of southern USA, therefore a westerner. I got raised a Christian, got educated, got rich compared to all those billions who make less than a thousand dollars a year. I am of the human species, an earthling, a universe person, first and last a creature of creation, and proud of it — but no more proud than all the other full-fledged members of creation. We are envied and enviable, each and every one of us.

Now, I can say I'm part of the human species, one of the youngest species. We are a Johnny-come-lately with a bighead thinking we are the best thing ever created. We have to make sure we don't let our children pick up such a myth. In one sense it's true, we are in the image of that which creates us. But our creation stories don't exactly say we are better than the next creature of creation. We have put our human spin on creation.

Genesis 1: "So God created human beings, making them to be like himself. . . . [L]ive all over the earth and bring it

under [your] control. I am putting you in charge"; Psalm
8: "[Y]ou made them [human beings] inferior only to
yourself;/ . . . You appointed them rulers over everything
you made;/ you placed them over all creation"; Protagoras
(c. 485-410 BCE): "Man is the measure of all things."

Augustine's spin is worse (maybe reflecting on Psalm 8)
when he said we are to "use" everything beneath us: there is God,
angels, humans, in that order; everything else is beneath us. In
other words, he thought some beings are better than others and
that we humans are definitely better than most everything else.

Well, western tradition, based on Augustine, Protagoras,
and biblical creation spins, is wrong. We are all "very good" —
including everything — created out of nothing by the mysterious
and loving power in the universe. Besides this, we want our
children to remember that each being was created of value. How
can we say anything is any better than anything else in creation?
The Sun is important, undoubtedly, but finally no more important
than the vegetables I ate last night for dinner. Einstein was right:
everything in being is as important as everything else because all
are held together as one thing — creation is one. Everything is
very good because it is blessed over and over again at creation
after creation.

Next, let me say I was dropped down the Christian well
into the one river of Spirit. Sure, I was raised a Christian, and
glad I was, though I decried the fact for a number of years. Is it
any better than other religions? No. Do Christians have any
privileged, inside information? No. Any edge on other religions?
No. Christianity is even younger than most, except Islam. I want
to be as clear as possible. I am not *just* a Christian. I am a religious
being, and *all* the stories of all religions of what it means to be
human and what it means to be a creature of creation are mine.

This makes me an aboriginal-Hindu-Buddhist-Confucian-
Taoist-Jain-Shintoist-Baha'i-Zoroastrian-Santerian-Jewish-

Muslim-Sikh-secularist Christian, and then some. All religious expressions are mine, each a petal of flower truth. Ownership is for the taking. Plagiarism is no problem here, for we are meant to borrow from the great wisdom and practices that make sense to us — a lavish religious smorgasbord. Take what helps you on the journey and be thankful to your forebears who put it on the table.

These religions are all human inventions, and since we're all humans reading this piece, then we can take and believe and practice any part of any religious well that takes us down to the one river of Spirit, for . . . all traditions are part of our one Spirit tradition. All the traditions of humanness belong to all the people. Let us stop being exclusive, righteous, and bigoted. No religion has all truth. No religion belongs to me and no religion belongs to you. All religions belong to all of us.

Why all the bigotry and religious wars for centuries? Why all the religious flexing of muscles of late? Maybe there is a lot of insecurity amongst our religions as we are exposed to each other's on this small planet. At any rate, I was raised a Christian bigot but am repenting. I am repenting of the fact that deep down I think my symbol system is better than others. I am repenting of being raised a Protestant who thinks I'm superior to Romans Catholics and Greek Orthodox. Are there not Buddhist, Jewish, and Muslim bigots who need to repent, also? Let us remember that such bigotry is the beginning of the religious wars past, present, and future that kill, maim, and destroy. Just ask them in Belfast, the Middle East, and Central Asia.

This brings us back to the big image above: we are all created equal (not just "all men are created equal"), all creatures of creation, first and last. As Berry says, "all elements of creation are not equal quantitatively as objects, but are equal qualitatively as subjects." Therefore, let us do away with bigotry in all religious traditions. Bigotry is one of our worst human inventions. Let us in our religious fervor kill *bigotry*, not each other. We religious should stand together if anybody does, knowing we are all persons led by Spirit, all part of the one reality that encounters, pervades, and connects us.

What is more fundamentally true than Spirit? This is the point I have been leading up to: we are one in Spirit. That is what *one river, many wells* means. So simple, so true, and so hard to keep in focus. Our oneness is because there is only one truth, one reality, one Spirit. If we are divided today, we are not in touch with the one Spirit.

When I talk about our Spirit tradition, I emphasize the word "our," meaning we all are children of the same Spirit; and meaning that in one sense it is contradictory to say "*my* Spirit tradition." Next, I emphasize the word "Spirit," not just any spirit with a small "s," but the one, true Spirit. Finally, I do *not* emphasize our sub-traditions, for example, Christianity or the West, but emphasize the *tradition of creation*, which also includes our human tradition with all its sub-traditions.

We are divided by species, race, nationality, class, sexual orientation, and religion. Community, from the family on out, is suffering. We intensify the destruction of humanity, our planet, and its environment daily. We are out of touch with Spirit. How do we rid ourselves of all the religious and cultural prejudices that divide us globally? This seems to be the question of the hour. How do we become united citizens of one Earth? Teilhard de Chardin points to a deep answer in the following quote:

> what is most vitally necessary to the thinking earth is a faith — and a great faith — and ever more faith . . . that if we are not to perish smothered in the very stuff of our being, is what we must at all costs secure.
> And it is there that we find what I may well be so bold as to call the *evolutionary role* of religions.[1]

We are looking for *a great faith* that makes sense to us in heart and head, that empowers us to spend ourselves for a peaceable kingdom on Earth, and by so doing be part of the next evolutionary leap. Key to this leap is the *evolutionary role of religions.* Teilhard knew his religious institution to be not very evolutionary: he was silenced by the Vatican from publishing anything but scientific writings for almost the last thirty years of his life, 1926-55.[2] Therefore, he especially yearned for a one-Spirit consciousness and a new spirit mode on the planet. He dedicated himself to that great cause through his writings, which have made him famous after his death.

We pray for Teilhard's zeal, for we too need to be in touch with *our one Spirit tradition* for creation's sake. We need only see and hear and be what we already are, one in Spirit. Let me say that over and over again until it becomes creation's ritual, "We are one in Spirit." Experiencing and believing this most important fact of our existence is our only conceivable way into the future.

so let us be
who we are

seamlessly
at one
with It

Verse 5

Spirit Makes the World Go Round

Cabaret says *money* makes the world go round
politicians say *power* makes the world go round
Hollywood says *entertainment* makes the world go round
education says *knowledge* makes the world go round
religion says *belief* makes the world go round

but Spirit makes the world go round
for Spirit encounters the big and the small
the rich and the poor
the educated and illiterate
the believing and unbelieving

why
to make us all grateful
for the way life is
even when we ain't got no
money
power
entertainment
knowledge
or
belief

—*september 2001*

Reflection 3

Spirit Makes the World Go Round:
A Hundred Ways

WHAT DO I MEAN BY "SPIRIT"? Even though the word is overused today, that isn't all bad if the users sense its deeply unifying power. In the back pages of my journal I have been listing descriptions of "Spirit." They are not all-inclusive but begin to communicate what I mean by the word "Spirit."

When I began this journal brainstorm, I was not so much interested in my more-than-a-hundred descriptions of the activity of Spirit as I was interested in the final number of categories they would gestalt into, ten, as it turned out. And then I was interested in the overall categories those ten would group into, four, as it turned out. So, you the reader need not be as concerned with the larger list as the smaller lists of ten and four. Maybe just scan and make notes in the margins of how Spirit acts in creation and your life experiences.

One more thing: these hundred ways Spirit works do not have to translate into a primarily human focus: the words "us," "we," and "our" *can* stand for all of us, not just humans or not even just sentient beings — but of course I don't understand how rocks and viruses respond to Spirit. Therefore, words like "conscious," "see," "experience," "reflect," and "decide" are used loosely.

I am very thankful that language is symbolic.

I. Spirit Happens

1.   Spirit is the source of creativity.
2.   Spirit is the essence of what is.
3.   Spirit is the deepening dimension in everything that is.
4.   Spirit is an event, first and foremost, that gets our attention.
5.   Spirit makes us sensitive to our actual situation.
6.   Spirit is to be sensed and experienced.
7.   Spirit reveals Itself; we do not find It.
8.   Spirit revelation is eternally here and now.
9.   Spirit moves us to experience the goodness of creation.

II. Spirit Awakens

10. Spirit awakens us eternally.
11. Spirit comes intuitively, usually through the ordinary.
12. Spirit awakens us to see the way life is and our true nature as at one with Its power.
13. Spirit communicates with the interior of all things.
14. Spirit awes and inspires.
15. Spirit sometimes overwhelms us with acceptance, love, and forgiveness.
16. Spirit enables us to say *Yes* to life as it is and our state of being as it is.
17. Spirit brings us to the miracle of faith in the goodness of the way life is.
18. Spirit increases consciousness, often at great pain.
19. Spirit is that which is always present, but certainly not always present in our awareness.
20. Spirit awakens us to Its eternal presence.

III. Spirit Frees

21. Spirit liberates us from separateness.

22. Spirit weans us from living out of some law so that we might live freely in our chosen obligations.
23. Spirit gives us the courage to risk.
24. Spirit allows us to choose to commune, yet is always forcing the issue.
25. Spirit is that dynamic that gives radical freedom, through our obligation to all that is, including our most microscopic and macroscopic neighbor.
26. Spirit calls forth decision, which is always free decision.

IV. Spirit Unites

27. Spirit is seamlessly at one with all that is.
28. Spirit intercommunes with all creation.
29. Spirit relates and unites the seemingly separate.
30. Spirit changes illusory separateness to authentic mutuality.
31. Spirit is always pushing us to be more inclusive.
32. Spirit brings us together.
33. Spirit bursts all boundaries, dumbfounds all assumptions.
34. Spirit shatters duality.
35. Spirit makes us at one with ongoing creation.
36. Spirit interconnects all that is.

V. Spirit Transforms

37. Spirit re-creates creation.
38. Spirit heightens our consciousness to care.
39. Spirit transforms I-it into I-Thou relationships.
40. Spirit births consciousness by allowing us not only to see the thing/situation itself, but also to reflect upon it, and to decide our relationship to it.
41. Spirit is an ever-present event that redeems the past.
42. Spirit manifests the essential nature or meaning of everything.

43. Spirit reveals creation to itself as it is and receives it just so.
44. Spirit reveals the infinite meaning of the finite.
45. Spirit opens our eyes to see life as good.
46. Spirit reveals to us our inner well-being.
47. Spirit reminds us that we who thirst are even now swimming in Its water, like fish.
48. Spirit allows us moments of transcendence.
49. Spirit reminds us that we are already what we seek to be, creatures of Spirit.

VI. Spirit Reconciles

50. Spirit fills us with transformative passion and compassion.
51. Spirit claims our gifts and technologies for comprehensive reconciliation.
52. Spirit confronts us with creation's pain.
53. Spirit gives us intimations for dealing with the urgencies of our times.
54. Spirit births love and responsibility for all creation.
55. Spirit calls/sends us to sacrifice ourselves on behalf of all.
56. Spirit reminds us that we are Its instruments, sent to remind others that they too are instruments of Spirit.
57. Spirit sanctifies simplicity so that all may simply live.
58. Spirit guides the great work within and by creation.
59. Spirit demands we unite or perish.

VII. Spirit Universalizes

60. Spirit is the dynamism in the universe.
61. Spirit is the "interior subjective numinous aspect of the entire cosmos."[1]
62. Spirit permeates all time-space-matter-energy reality.
63. Spirit is everywhere at every time and experienced by all creation.

64. Spirit hides within every dimension of the universe.
65. Spirit and matter are forever entwined.
66. Spirit sustains us through community, the Earth being our biggest (if not the Milky Way Galaxy, if not the universe, if not the multiverse).
67. Spirit reveals Itself to us through the processes of the Earth, since we are earthlings.
68. Spirit enables the Earth to become conscious of itself as one being.
69. Spirit makes us aware of our wounded and broken Earth body and calls us to be about its healing.
70. Spirit reveals to all a birthright and liferight.
71. Spirit is prior to cultural and sacred traditions and is always pushing them to be more universal.
72. Spirit is the inner-being/inter-being dynamic of all being.

VIII. Spirit Enlightens

73. Spirit opens us to possibilities that thrill and terrify us.
74. Spirit reveals Itself without ceasing, whether It is perceived or not.
75. Spirit has no levels and cannot to be developed.
76. Spirit tags "spiritual development" an illusion: we can only develop consciousness of Spirit.
77. Spirit calls us to live in the present rather than in expectation or memory.
78. Spirit is omnipresent.
79. Spirit sometimes comes as illumination.
80. Spirit reminds us that we are Its sensors.
81. Spirit cannot be fully experienced nor expressed.
82. Spirit communes with us.

IX. Spirit Sustains

83. "Spirit is always already present" yet seemingly always escaping.
84. Spirit never lets us go but always lets us be.
85. Spirit assures inherent quality of life.
86. Spirit soothes our suffering and pain.
87. Spirit constantly grows us by transcending us.
88. Spirit enfolds us by allowing us to participate in Its creation.
89. Spirit lures us to intercommunion with all that is.
90. Spirit journeys us.

X. Spirit Reigns

91. Spirit fills the whole universe, supplying "the juice of life" to all.
92. Spirit confirms that we, and everything that is, are Spirit motivated.
93. Spirit is not made in our image, but creation is in Spirit's image.
94. Spirit cannot be compelled to do anything.
95. Spirit convinces us that we are hardly divine, but in touch with divinity.
96. Spirit announces that Its Kingdom is within creation.
97. Spirit makes its home where It wills, even in the soul.[2]
98. Spirit reminds us that we and everything else are transparent to It.
99. Spirit is the most powerful dynamic in creation.
100. Spirit commissions all to be on the spirit journey.

These descriptions lead me to say "Spirit makes the world go round." From this brainstorm of one-hundred and gestalt of ten, one can begin to see an overall frame for the way Spirit acts. These ten groups easily make four overarching categories:

Interior Spirit Dynamics

I. *Spirit Happens,* II. *Spirit Awakens,* and III. *Spirit Frees*

Exterior Spirit Dynamics

IV. *Spirit Unites,* V. *Spirit Transforms,* and VI. *Spirit Reconciles*

Universal Spirit Dynamics

VII. *Spirit Universalizes,* VIII. *Spirit Enlightens,* and
IX. *Spirit Sustains*

Omnipotent Spirit Dynamics

X. *Spirit Reigns*

*****

As far as we humans are concerned —

> from our (130,000 or) 40,000 year history as modern
>   Homo sapiens[3]
> from our 2.6 million year history as humans
> from our 5-7 million year history as pre-humans
> from our 4.7 billion year history as Earth, or
> from our 13-14.6 billion year history as universe

— whichever number one likes best in dating our history — we are what we are primarily because of the activity of Spirit and our response to It. I will even say we are Spirit beings, for Spirit is more constant in our human journeys than our some 100,800 heartbeats a day.

Furthermore, creation is being driven by, responding to, and giving thanks for (or cursing) Spirit, the deepest reality we all have in common. Spirit truly is creation's ground of being and ground of meaning. *Spirit makes the world go round.*

Spirit is the primal and awesome activity of our one spiritual tradition. Therefore, it seems foolish for us to try to squeeze ourselves and others into any particular spiritual tradition. It does not finally matter if we come to a good relationship with creation and Spirit through Abraham, Jesus, Buddha, Muhammed, or Lao-Tzu so long as we know that Spirit and creation love us and that we are here to love Spirit and creation back.[4]

Verse 6

Spiritually Correct

Does it matter
what we call iT
so long as we unite

Whether we call iT
>*Spirit*
>*God*
>*One*
>*Ultimate*
>*Numinous*
>*Father*
>*Goddess*
>*Emptiness*

we bow before that mysterious power
blowing this way and that
sometimes at our back
sometimes in our faces
but always stirring
whether we sense it or not

Language is hardly the message
only a medium of expression
of what we perceive
>images
>poetry
>metaphor

our way
to say something
about what we see
intuit
experience

Our words are not iT
even holy writ
only inklings
and intimations

The message is
always
written on the wind
sometimes in-
spiring the heart

Therefore,
to be
spiritually correct
unite in
iTs presence

—*february 2001*

Reflection 4

Spirituality:
Intercommunion as the Way of Life

Verse 7   *Spirituality Is*

spirituality reflects Spirit in the pool of one's inner life

spirituality reflects Spirit in the prism of one's outer life

spirituality is the universal journey of existence

spirituality is seeing the numinous power energizing life

spirituality is living in the memory of awe-filled moments

spirituality is the knowledge of unitive truth

spirituality is the origin of religions

spirituality is fulfilling the heart's desire

spirituality is the seat of creativity

spirituality is manifest in sacrificial living

spirituality is manifest in a life-style of local and
    universal service

spirituality is the experience of mystery, lucidity,
    love, and tranquility

spirituality is the experience of care, grace, freedom,
        and compassion

spirituality is the being of knowing and doing

spirituality is the universal experience of relating to Spirit

spirituality is the circumference, height, and depth
        of our relationships

spirituality is an *I-Thou* relationship with all that is

                              *****

spirituality is not only an inner experience of union
but also a union with creation's outer universe, earth,
humanity, that demonstrates passionate care

spirituality is the experience of at-one-ment with Spirit in life,
not an attempted identity with It or control of It

*spirituality is not so much a divine-human affair in which Spirit
is present primarily in the human realm*
as it is a divine-universe affair in which Spirit is present in the
universe realm, which includes the human

spirituality is not a mystical relationship
unless it is also a relationship of union with the universe

*spirituality is not so much a looking for Spirit,
        assuming Spirit is absent,*
as it is an awareness of Spirit, assuming Spirit is present

spirituality is not only meditation and prayer
but also contemplation of the universe

*spirituality is not so much an effort to achieve
        union with anything*

as it is our *Yes* to grace happening in our universe

spirituality is not only an interior state of being
but also a sacramental mode of living[1]

*****

spirituality is being encountered by Spirit and saying *Yes*,
thankfully and obediently — "If they ask what I did well,/
tell them I said, 'Yes,' to life"[2]

spirituality is saying *Yes* to Spirit in life that re-births,
re-images, re-arranges, re-directs, re-motivates

—*december 2000*

SPIRITUALITY IS NO MORE ABOUT THE INTERIOR LIFE than the exterior life. One's whole life is a translucent veil covering one's spirituality. Spirituality is a universal mark of being. Spirituality is no longer reserved for the devout and the mystics. Spirituality is no more religious than secular. As Kabir wrote,

> you will not find me . . . in Indian shrine
> rooms, nor in synagogues, nor in cathedrals. . . .
> When you really look for me, you will see me
> instantly. . . .
> [I am] the breath inside the breath.[3]

Spirituality is about all our relationships, not just a relationship with the divine. I'd rather say divinity is at the center of all relationships; therefore, spirituality is the journey of seeing our relationships with creation as sacred: the relationship with the universe, with planet Earth, with all species, with humans near and far, from our family to our so-called enemies. Spirituality is our way of sensing after the profound energizing dimension of creation and relating to it meaningfully, mysterious as it is.

Ken Wilber is the pioneer in post-metaphysical spirituality for our time, comprehensively charting twelve stages, with four states each (or a total of up to forty-eight). He says Spirit is the Ground of all levels.[4] Spirit

> allows somebody [anybody, even children] at virtually any stage of development to find some degree of realization and enlightenment . . . — whether a thousand years ago, today, or a thousand years hence. These timeless, spaceless, formless aspects of Spirit . . . appear to be part of Spirit's ever-present grace. . . .[5]

Nicolai Hartmann said there are four strata of being: 1) the physical, 2) the biological (or organic), 3) the conscious (or psychic), and 4) the spiritual. Though he does not talk about "spiritual" as I do, his observation of the four makes sense to me, especially since many would equate spirit with consciousness or psyche; he and I do not. Consciousness and psyche are certainly sensors of Spirit. The fourth strata, "spiritual," is the apogee of Hartmann's list, but makes itself known in and through them.[6] Spirit is the depth energy of the one reality that makes the world go round in one amazing, swirling-dervish creation, and, therefore, spirituality is about the journey of being in sync with all that.

Being in touch with Spirit is being brought to consciousness. Consciousness is a state of being aware that is triggered or happens. If I become conscious of Spirit in an awesome moment, then "consciousness" and "Spirit" are not the same. Spirit facilitates consciousness. To refer to Spirit as consciousness is not helpful — I fear that much of the spiritual teaching and writing of our day is confused at this point. For me, Spirit is that Power encountering my life day to day, in the events of 9/11, being kissed by my grandchildren, or enthralled by the moon

— whether I'm seeking Its presence or not. Spirit is wild and not to be domesticated. "It blows where it will." Spirit is different from me — and my consciousness — but it encounters me.

Therefore, *being in touch with Spirit* is being made conscious of that in life which I can embrace or deny: for example, the gifts and un-gifts of my aging. The Spirit question that delivers us into our freedom of choice asks each of us most directly, Will you or won't you have this situation (e.g., aging) as it is? *Yea* or *nay*? Which is it? And that is not what we usually think of as "raised consciousness." Spirit more often than not comes to us in an encounter we feel at the time we can definitely do without.

Having said this much about spirituality, I admit its prevailing mystery. Consequently, I resort to poetry and art to help image what this reality of realities is.

A Sufi parable illumines the mystery of spirituality. In a great banquet everyone was seated according to rank, awaiting the entry of the King. In came a plain, shabby man and took a seat above everyone else. His boldness angered the first minister, who ordered the newcomer to identify himself.

> "Are you a minister?"
> "No. More," replied the poor man.
> "Are you the King?"
> "No. More."
> "Are you God?" asked the prime minister, losing patience.
> "I am also above God," answered the poor man.
> "There is nothing above God!" retorted the prime minister.
> "Right. That 'nothing' is what I am," said the poor man.

The poor man understood what it is to be on the journey of spirituality: everyone is of greatest significance and everyone is of the same rank — definitely a paradox for us today in our class and caste consciousness, but more especially among those who consider themselves to be religious and spiritual. The truth is it is impossible for anyone to be closer to Spirit than anyone else. Because Spirit is, and everyone is related to It equally, all are on the one, same spirit journey. The prime minister was living out of illusion because he did not see this relational truth of spirituality that the poor man saw: our equality in spirit and Spirit's closeness to each of us. Both are our source of humility. Simply, we are Spirit's creatures.

The "Trans-" Character of Spirituality

In addition to the "transrelational" aspect of spirituality above — all things are related to Spirit and therefore all things are related to each other — let's describe this mysterious journey we are all on using other words beginning with "trans-": transparent, transrational, transpersonal, transvalued, transestablished, and transformed.

The "transparent" journey is about our seeing what is really going on in life at a deeper level, or seeing the extraordinary in the ordinariness of existence, or seeing through to the heart of things. This is what spirituality is about.

Spirituality is a "transrational" experience. Ken Wilber says that in reality there is a "seamless union of transcendental and empirical, other-worldly and this-worldly. For the higher levels themselves are not *above* the natural or empirical or objective, they are *within* the natural and empirical and objective."[7] He uses another, even professional, word for this perception: "transpersonal," the every-person experience of spirituality that is not limited to rational, scientific knowledge; or Spirit is the integer of everything and therefore transrationalizes or "transvalues" everything in Its meeting.

"Transestablishment" is a word that bridges the establishment and the disestablishment in society. It holds the understanding for spirituality that what we are about on the journey is not seeing things as separate but as one. Spirit thereby "transforms" our outer relationships as we go about the living venture of honoring and reconciling all things.

The Being of Knowing and Doing

Spirituality is the frame of our everyday knowing and doing. We do not have to go somewhere or do something special to find the meaning of life. Life is at the center of living. We do not have to believe in some deity, for example, to live spiritually. In fact, belief often clouds our seeing. Simply,

> if we see in the chewing of food the wonder of taste
> if we see in our associations the wonder of being together
> if we see in the meteor shower the wonder of the cosmos
> if we see in our grandchildren the wonder of their wonder
> if we see in 9/11 events the wonder of our precious finitude
> if we see in dreaming the wonder of imagination
> if we see in sexuality the wonder of attraction and union
> if we see in birth and death the wonder of life

then we begin to get it, this thing called spirituality, the way of life that is intercommunion for all created subjects who are given to see to the heart of what is. Spirituality is not just for the religious but is for everyone. Spirituality points to the being of knowing, that seeing the truth makes us at one with truth.

Likewise, if we see in our doing the wonder of creativity, or if we see in our doing the wonder of intercommunion and service, we are on the way of being, on the way of spirituality. D. H. Lawrence understands spirituality, even though he was kicked out of his religious institution:

> As we live, we are transmitters of life.
> And when we fail to transmit life, life fails to flow through us. . . .
> And if, as we work, we can transmit life into our work,
> life, still more life, rushes into us to compensate, to be ready

and we ripple with life through the days.

Even if it is a woman making an apple dumpling,
        or a man a stool,
if life goes into the pudding, good is the pudding
good is the stool,
content is the woman, with fresh life rippling in to her,
content is the man.

Give, and it shall be given unto you
Is still the truth about life. . . .
It means kindling the life-quality where it was not,
Even if it's only in the whiteness of a washed
        pocket-handkerchief.[8]

The poet understands that everyday life is the medium of spirituality. He understands that Being is at the heart of work, that the "life-quality" shows up in the spirituality that is life. We find Being (Spirit) in our knowing and doing when we *see* and *transmit life*, for Being is everywhere already, waiting and "ready to . . . ripple with life through the days." We can block it or transmit it through our living.

Communicating the Truth

There is another dimension that cannot be left out of this reflection, lest we reduce spirituality to egoism or warm feelings. Wilber reminds us of the *bodhisattva* vow of ancient India's spirituality:

> You were allowed to see the truth under the agreement that you would communicate it to others. . . . And therefore, if you have seen, you simply must speak out. . . . [Only by speaking what you have seen] with passion, can the truth . . . finally penetrate the reluctance of the world. . . . [I]t is your duty to speak your truth with whatever passion and courage you can find in your heart.[9]

To speak the truth through our words and through our lives is the obligation that authenticates spirituality in us humans. Healthy spirituality flows in and out with passion. Is that passionate, in-and-out flow happening through us or are our spirits clogged? is the truth-question of our lives.

Spirituality is mysterious, but this we do know: spirituality is the way wherein we experience vitality, truth, and transformation. What is the source? The "breath inside the breath" says Kabir (15th century), "life rippling in" says Lawrence (20th century), "Spirit's ever-present grace" says Wilber (21st century). Therefore, we are all on Spirit's journey.

Reflection 5

Life Pictures:
Where Does Spirit Fit In?

EACH OF US OPERATES OUT OF A LIFE PICTURE. To most of us, this picture of life from beginning to end is not clear. Yet, intimations come now and again to inform our journey. Let us consider a dozen or so life pictures to get more clarity on our own journey and where Spirit fits in.

> *King Sisyphus* ended up in Hades
> to eternally roll a huge rock up a long, steep hill,
> only to watch it roll back down the same side.
> For him demands are unending,
> thankless, and end in unsuccessful efforts.
> He might well have said, "This is not fair."
> Or, "The gods are against me."
> Or, "What's the use?"
> For Sisyphus life is hell to live.
> > Where is Spirit? Just over the hill?

> *King Tantalus*, another king who offended the gods,
> also paid the price in Hades.
> He was condemned to stand beneath fruit-laden boughs,
> up to his chin in water.
> Whenever he bent his head to drink, the water receded,
> and whenever he reached for the fruit, the branches moved
> > beyond his grasp.
> Thus to "tantalize" is to tease or torment
> by offering something desirable but keeping it out of reach.

For Tantalus, too, life is hell to live.
          Where is Spirit? Just out of reach?

Rich Man had much land and better than usual crops,
so he decided to build bigger barns to store his goods.
He said, "When my barns are full I will take life easy
          and celebrate."
Anxious about the future he was not merry yet.
Jesus said God called Rich Man a fool. Why?
Was it because he would build even more barns next year?
Was it because his life was under siege by
          the unknown future?
Or was it because he spent his life now securing life
          in the future?
In any case, Rich Man's life was spent, for that night he died.
          Where is Spirit? At some future celebration?

Then there was *Faust*, who wanted a monument
erected to his creativity.
As an old, blind man he heard clanking
          outside his window.
He thought they were completing his monument, finally.
Instead, they were digging his grave.
Life for him was all about carving his name on the future,
consecrating his great knowing and doing.
But Faust too was a fool
for wanting his name to never die.
          Where is Spirit? In our great accomplishments?

But all these fools were from the more distant past.
Are there any alive in our day?
Yes, there is *Lester* in the movie *American Beauty*,
the pitiful, middle-aged man played by Kevin Spacey.
Some think he was redeemed when he got freed up
and did what felt good no matter whom it hurt.
But, alas, that smile on his face toward his tragic end

was hardly the smile of one who has come through.
Maybe, like Faust, he too was caught up in his ego needs.
          Where is Spirit? In selfish lust for freedom?

Or consider *Melvin* (Jack Nicholson) in *As Good As It Gets*.
What a fool he was flaunting his neuroses
          all over Manhattan:
hating dogs, gays, women, Jews — and himself.
But he became attached to a little dog, befriended
          his gay neighbor,
fell in love with his waitress, Carol (Helen Hunt),
and paid the doctor to cure her son.
Melvin and Carol both got awakened event after event,
until they began to see that their lives separately
and together were as good as they were going to get.
          Where is Spirit? In the little big events of life?

Life is Beautiful, starring Roberto Benigni as *Guido*,
is another movie that won many Oscars.
It too is about a foolish man who bumps into creation,
and who in spite of himself
finds a wonderful woman and their son to love.
This outrageous man proclaims life is good,
even in a Nazi death camp in Italy,
in one huge masquerade after another to save his young son.
For Guido, all of life is a play.
          Where is Spirit? In the role one is given to enact?

A more recent Academy Award winner,
          Erin Brockovich (Julia Roberts).
She was a fool whose life and family were coming apart,
when a legal case-and-a-half bumped into her:
contaminated water runoff from Pacific Gas and
          Electric's plant.
She helped prove they were knowingly liable to tens of
          families living nearby.

This woman's passion rose in relation to
the compassion she felt visiting and befriending the victims.
She became their champion and PG&E's worst nightmare.
See what one broken-down woman can do when motivated.
        Where is Spirit? Born of compassion?

An older Academy Award winner was *Zorba* (Anthony Quinn),
who like Faust wanted to build a monument.
His was a conveyor from the mine
down the hill to the coast for the minerals to be shipped.
Trestles and railway installed, they cut the ribbon on the first run.
But the full wagons rolling down set off vibrations
        in the total structure.
It fell apart, piece by piece, until it all piled on the
        ground demolished.
Silence, end of a dream, and Zorba broke down and cried?
Hardly. He began the dance he became famous for,
        a more fitting monument.
        Where is Spirit? In the celebration of life and death?

Consider those who lived and died in Nazi death camps.
Victor Frankl watched and reflected on
the ways his fellow Jewish prisoners dealt
        with their holocaust.
What amazed and changed him was their undying spirit.
Many truly lived in the hope that the Sun
        would come up tomorrow
or in the remembered image of the *Thou* of a loved one.
At another camp was a young woman named *Elly Hillesum,*
who became a saint as she prepared to go to the gas chamber.
Among her last words: "I vow to live my life out there to the full."
        Where is Spirit? In any conceivable situation?

As we consider saints and martyrs,
what about *Gandhi,* who was a different kind of lawyer,
one who used his legal savvy to confound

the South African government on behalf of all "colored"
and to liberate his homeland from oppressive British rule.
His nonviolent ideology and movement reverberated
into the life of young *Martin Luther King, Jr.,*
as he and colleagues brought the Birmingham system to its knees
and helped change the laws of his homeland.
>Where is Spirit? Hiding in social injustices of our time?

Likewise, consider *Desmond Tutu* of South Africa,
who helped conceive and implement
the most daring secular forgiveness structure of our time:
the Truth and Reconciliation Commission,
wherein some 21,000 victims of apartheid gave testimony,
and over 7000 perpetrators confessed and sought forgiveness.
Thousands on both sides were changed demonstrably
>by forgiveness.

This model of dealing with the wounded histories of nations
has spread beyond S. A., honoring a deeper law than on the books.
>Where is Spirit? In forgiveness and reconciliation?

And let me introduce one of my favorite friends,
Shakuntalah Belge Jadhav of Pune, India.
I first met her when she was about nineteen-years-old,
beginning to lead human development programs
>across the State of Maharashtra.

She has spent her last twenty-some years giving herself
by living with, motivating, and training thousands of villagers
to pick up their villages and their lives
and to walk into the future with their heads held high.
She is now sick with cancer, but has not stopped her great work.
>Where is Spirit? In spending self on behalf of others?

Thomas Berry, now at eighty-seven years of age,
is spending his life brooding over how we care for creation.
His witness through his teaching and books
has brought us a new vision for the Earth,

a new picture of the universe,
a new role for the human,
and a definition of *the great work* awaiting us:
the mutual care by all for all.
As I write, he is preparing another book.
                Where is Spirit? In loving creation?

THESE LIFE PICUTRES are a short listing of how and where
Spirit fits into our lives. Reflect again on each of the questions
after "Where is Spirit?"

- Just over the hill?
- Just out of reach?
- At some future celebration?
- In our great accomplishments?
- In selfish lusts for freedom?
- In the little big events of life?
- In the role one is given to enact?
- Born of compassion?
- In the celebration of life and death?
- In any conceivable situation?
- Hiding in the social injustices of our time?
- In social forgiveness and reconciliation?
- In expending oneself on behalf of others?
- In loving creation?

Our answer to Where is Spirit? makes all the difference
to the way we live our lives. Spirit leavens our existence. If
Spirit is seen as absent or relegated to some future existence,
we miss fulfillment in this life. If our life picture tells us Spirit is
present, then it's a matter of how we respond to its presence, as
a blessing or curse. Spirituality hinges on our answer to the
question of where is Spirit in our life picture.

"Spirit" Etymology

Spirit is the heart of creation
Spirit never stops creating
Spirit dynamizes process
Spirit ennobles existence
Spirit lets loose grace
Spirit births holiness

creation is a piece of work
creation never stops creating
creation is in process
creation is good
creation is gracious
creation is holy

life is a piece of creation
life never stops creating
life is in process
life is good
life is gracious
life is holy

almost seems natural
to love life
and all creation
since *Spirit*
tran-spires[1]
and *in-spires*[2]

such is the history
of this word *spiritus*[3]
'a fine wind is blowing'

—*february 2001*

1 Reveals. 2 Enlivens, motivates. 3 Breath of life and creation.

"Sacred Moment" by Ellen Howie

Section Two

The Dynamics of Transparency

In Section Two we will focus upon spirit dynamics as we humans experience and perceive them. We will look at the four dynamics of the *Other World* (in the midst of this world) *Charts*: I. The Land of Mystery, II. The River of Consciousness, III. The Mountain of Care, and IV. The Sea of Tranquility. The dynamics resonate with the ten brainstorm clusters and one-hundred descriptions in Reflection 3.

Mystery:
X. Spirit Reigns and I. Spirit Happens

Consciousness:
II. Spirit Awakens, V. Spirit Transforms, and III. Spirit Frees

Care:
VII. Spirit Universalizes and VI. Spirit Reconciles

Fulfillment/Tranquility:
VIII. Spirit Enlightens, IV. Spirit Unites, and IX. Spirit Sustains

Verse 9

Is Spirit Real?

Which is more real . . .

> . . . birth of my sons or death of my parents?
> . . . love of peace or fear of war?
> . . . scientific fact or theoretical concept?
> . . . poetic image or meticulous description?
> . . . truth or illusion?
> . . . experience or intuition?
> . . . risk or security?
> . . . event or story?
> . . . faith or miracle?

Which is less real . . .

> . . . proof or ambiguity?
> . . . commitment or detachment?
> . . . feeling or calculation?
> . . . decision or intention?
> . . . vision or plan?
> . . . subjectivity or objectivity?
> . . . light or dark?
> . . . belief or fantasy?
> . . . feast or famine?
> . . . doubt or certainty?
> . . . laughter or tears?

Which is really real . . .

> . . . mental image or photograph?
> . . . inclusiveness or exclusiveness?
> . . . childhood or age?
> . . . a rose or a thorn?
> . . . chocolates or fasting?
> . . . a kiss or a snub?
> . . . consciousness or unconsciousness?
> . . . time or space?
> . . . past or future?
> . . . sound or silence?
> . . . dream or actuality?

When was the last time I experienced something real?

Have I experienced . . .

> . . . beginning and ending?
> . . . fullness and emptiness?
> . . . memory and being present?
> . . . sadness and joy?
> . . . intimacy and wonder?
> . . . boredom and mission?
> . . . fear and comfort?
> . . . power and weakness?

Have I experienced . . .

> . . . despair and tranquility?
> . . . pain and pleasure?
> . . . estrangement and reunion?
> . . . it-ness and thou-ness?

... forgiveness and separation?
... dread and hope?
... heart and soul?
... greatness and depth?

Have I experienced . . .

... closed down and opened up?
... freedom and imprisonment?
... dead right and dead wrong?
... imagination and vacuity?
... dead end and new life?
... last chance and second chance?
... raging storm and gentle breeze?
... twilight and dawn?
... mystery and awe?

What have I experienced?
What is real?
What does all this have to do with Spirit?
Is reality what I think it is?

What is really happening?
How to test reality?
The real reality?
Living reality?

Read it again and cogitate — What is real?
What have I experienced?
Has Spirit happened to me or not?
Is Spirit real?

—*november 2001*

Verse 10

The Way Spirit Works

The way Spirit works is not the way the tradition says:
A power from outside this world enters it and makes something happen.
That is otherworldly magic, which went out of vogue sometime ago.
Spirit is always *of* and *for* this world — and *by?*
I guess It comes from the same place everything else comes from.

Son John received this e-mail from a friend in Indonesia:
"rella gave birth last night: aruna francisca, 44 cm, 2.25 kg. . . .
it was pretty amazing this morning to hold her in my arms.
i looked up at the sky last night while waiting,
and i was wondering if there was anything up there
        besides greenhouse gases.
looking at her little face was like seeing the universe and
knowing that it is good. ~regards, jiway"

At such awesome moments of "looking at her little face,"
We create words like "wonder" and "awesome."
We may look to the heavens, but we know where these
        phenomena come from —
"Like seeing the universe" reveal its heart and "knowing that it is good."
Gracious moments give us a peek at the way Spirit works.

—*july 2001*

Verse 11

bet you've experienced It

"What'd ya mean, 'transparency'?"
Let the poetry wash over you . . .

I saw the light . . . blind but now I see . . . been to the mountain
. . . wow . . . happy day . . . the be-all and end-all . . . turning
point . . . it all came together . . . alignment . . . in the zone . . .
meaning bleeding from every moment . . . new vision . . .
ephiphany . . . sacred moment . . . inspired . . . transformed . . .
transfixed . . . this is the time . . . this is the place . . . rang my
chime . . . red alert . . . advent . . . cataclysmic . . . defining
moment . . . before and after . . . dead man walking . . . scales
falling from my eyes . . . bowled over . . . great god a'mighty,
free at last . . . synchronicity . . . gestalt . . . eureka . . . aha . . .
overwhelmed . . . assaulted . . . awesome encounter . . . terrifying
. . . blown apart . . . life changing . . . rose up a new man . . .
kairotic . . . resurrected . . . grace . . . took off my shoes . . . holy
ground . . . at the center . . . called . . . I'm the one . . . we're
it . . . the Hesperides . . . kingdom come on earth . . . strange
peace . . . miraculous . . . the great event

. . . like songwriters, I sometimes "see through" . . .

what a wonderful world . . . zipadeedooda . . . my or my, what a
wonderful day . . . goodness gracious, great balls of fire . . . lightning
moment, blazing spark . . . the lightning of his terrible swift sword
. . . I'm going to Graceland . . . I know what I know . . . lost in a
sweet place . . . all is well . . . I surrender . . . celebrate . . . wade

in the water . . . I found you just in time . . . everything is satisfaction . . . it's a grand night for singing . . . the earth is aglow . . . never saw things going so right . . . there's wonder in most everything I see . . . does enchantment pour out of every door . . . there's nowhere else on earth that I would rather be . . . I could have danced all night . . . my heart took flight . . . oh what a beautiful morning . . . all the sounds of the earth are like music . . . on a clear day how it will astound you . . . that the glow of your being outshines every star . . . you can see forever and ever and evermore . . . the trumpets of glory now call me to ride . . . whithersoever they blow, onward to glory I go

. . . sometimes these common, popular words make sense when I experience the

> *primal*
> *life-changing*
> *secular-religious*
> *other-world-in-this-world*

events of life. . . .

That's what I mean by "transparency."
Bet you've experienced It.

—april 2002

Reflection 6

Transparency:
The Other World in This World

Matter is transparent . . . in relation to spirit.[1]
~Teilhard de Chardin

Spirit rushes, storms through matter and fructifies it. . . .
It molds us, pummels matter within us and turns it into
spirit.[2] **~Nikos Kazantzakis**

What is needed, then, is a *new other-worldliness* . . . [a]
post-liberal . . . attack on pure secularism.[3]
~H. Richard Niebuhr

¶ Probably the biggest contradiction in our time is the absence of
an adequate mythology whereby we have a roadmap over and
through the terrain, the topography, of the Other World [in the
midst of This World].
¶ In our time we have succeeded rather admirably in destroying the
two-story universe [the Other World apart from This World].
¶ When you talk about the Other World, you are dealing with the ordinary
secular world and secular human consciousness.
¶ The *transparency* of this one world is *the new metaphysics.*
¶ A state of being, a state of awareness, a state of consciousness is the
most objective reality that one ever experiences.
¶ The poetry [we are inventing] . . . is a new mythology that will enable
us to find our way to swim [and not drown], if you please, in the rivers
of radical consciousness and become human.[4]
~Joseph W. Mathews

AS MORE AND MORE PEOPLE ARE TURNED OFF by the otherworldliness of religions, especially over the past three hundred years, spiritual bankruptcy is the cost: life perceived as uneventful, so we entertain ourselves without ceasing; life perceived as not meaningful, not fulfilling, so we commit strung-out suicide; life perceived as a "wasteland," so we waste life and creation.

Or take for example the suicidal hijackers of 9/11, who understood that they would be rewarded with virgins in heaven if they did the deed in the name of Allah. Spirituality has become too much the property of otherworldly groups, be they Muslim or Christian fundamentalists. This has to stop. Spirituality is not otherworldly and is not the property of anyone, but is here and now and the birthright of all. The masses must rediscover that Spirit is in this one-and-only world, not in some other world before, above, beyond, or in the future.

Since the 17th century Cartesian paradigm, and before with the Greeks and Persians, a dualistic notion has led to the great split between matter and Spirit. Matter has captured the domain of the "real world" for us since. In the West, in our rebellion against the tyranny of institutional religion and its otherworldly dogmas, spirituality was lumped with magic and mythology as otherworldly and was thrown out with religion by the Enlightenment.

Secularism has been winning the day with its nonreligious, one-world understanding of existence, which is absolutely true and absolutely false. It is true that this is the life we have, between birth and death, the time of consciousness. It is absolutely *not* true that Spirit is otherworldly. The truth is that our lives between birth and death are the domain of the Spirit, or as Zen Buddhism would say, Spirit is all about sanctifying the ordinary: "At this very moment one partakes of Eternal Life."[5] Spirit is in this world, or *the other world is in the midst of this world.* Spirit is here and now, or nowhere that we can experience. Let me be as emphatic as I can: heaven, nirvana, paradise, utopia, bliss — all are here and now in this world, in this life — and transparently so.

Transparency

Joseph W. Mathews and the Order and the Institutes, through the development of a context and practical methods, began to give flesh to the self-understanding that the other world is in this world. We were passionate about the self-understanding and methods that would allow persons to experience Spirit at the center of their lives.

Mathews used the word "transparent" to designate the dynamic of Spirit in this world. H. Richard Niebuhr and Søren Kierkegaard were key sources, the latter writing, "By relating itself to its own self and by willing to be itself, the self is grounded *transparently* in the Power which posited it."[6]

"Transparent" and "transparency" are helpful words, not conventional terms people think they understand. The word "transparent" is rich in meaning, coming from "to show through"; "fine or sheer enough to be seen through," "revealing," "capable of transmitting light," "translucent," "readily understood," "true"; sometimes the connotation of "lighted from the inside."

"Transparency," then, is pointing to the understanding of the Spirit as having no particular content ("contentless," Mathews' word) — "universal" is another way to say it. Transparency describes a dynamic of the way life is for everyone: at times one can see clearly life's reality, as through a clear window pane. Or everyone has experienced bursts of consciousness that make the moment full and meaningful. In the midst of ordinary life comes the transparent event of Spirit that alters consciousness, decision, and even life-style. Afterwards one understands that Spirit is at the heart of all and is always present. So Spirit is transparent, eventful, contentless, universal, dynamic, and transformative.

Mathews liked to say "the messiah has already come" for every person. Stop the quest. Open your eyes and see. Speaking out of the Judaic-Christian tradition, he said, "The Christ decision was *transparently* an election for or against life itself. The negative answer was at bottom a rejection of human existence as it is constituted."[7] Here the word "transparently" means that which reveals "human existence as it is constituted," good as it has always been. The twist is that we humans are seldom aware of existence as it is constituted; we become numb to it, or we cover it up because we perceive it as bad to us the way it is. In which case, something must happen to us to uncover what is forgotten or covered up.

In this context, Spirit delivers to us life's ultimate question: Is life — and my life — good or bad the way it is? This question will not go away. From this we must question any religious tradition's understanding: Is it true to life? Do the dynamics come out of life or are they superimposed upon the way life is? The way life is, is the key to interpreting truth. Why in the world would some god create the way life is in the beginning — as perfectly good — and then come along and create another set of life dynamics for this or that religion: for example, life is basically bad? The way life is, is the way life is. If it's good in the beginning, as the story says, then it's good all the way through. Religions at their best have given us the understanding of the way life is in its essence as good.

The transparent Spirit dynamic is captured in these lines from my favorite song, "What a Wonderful World," sung by Louis Armstrong, my favorite jazz musician and singer. My son Jeremiah, over twelve years ago, rigged my computer so Louis sings this refrain as I boot up:

> I see skies of blue
> and clouds of white,
> the bright, blessed day,

> the dark, sacred night,
> and I think to myself,
> 'What a wonderful world!'[8]

In looking up the writer of the song, I ran across this unbelievable lesson on the web from pastor so-and-so:

> Now to this week's [music] selection, "What a Wonderful World." Even the Junior Bible Bombers [what a name!] . . . know better than to say this! God warns us repeatedly not to be of the world, and that by doing so we are of all men most miserable (1 Cor. 15:19). He states that the world is evil and will eventually be destroyed. Our eyes should not be focused on the frivolities of everyday existence. We are to look to the Father, and to the day that we will leave this world and spend eternity in God's kingdom, where we will be free from sin and Satan's influence. To blissfully gaze upon mankind and his worldly creations and "think to yourself, what a wonderful world" has no place in the life of a believer.

This type of thinking is what I call bad spirituality because it is not in touch with the way life is, good as given. It can result in all sorts of disrelations born of its principles: the Earth is of no value; the world and we are evil and therefore will be destroyed; everyday existence is frivolous; we are to wait on the Lord, just wait; prepare to leave this world to spend eternity in God's kingdom beyond this world — God's kingdom is not here, only Satan's; "God" is a person and a "He."

Pastor so-and-so's two-story, otherworldly theology does not make sense to most people I know. Out of my experience, he is wrong about my favorite song quoted above, which suggests another understanding of life: essentially, the life I see is transparent to the goodness of life. Mother Teresa was enabled to see transparently that the poor and dying on the streets of Calcutta are "children of God" and therefore have a right to a sacred place and way to die. Archbishop Tutu saw transparently that the perpetrators of the atrocities in South Africa are worthy of forgiveness. When a bad situation goes transparent to "a wonderful world," it transforms consciousness and generates new creation.

Maybe pastor so-and-so does not believe in resurrection or new life. He obviously thinks they are *not* part of this world. His metaphysics is full of illusion. I do not want to sign up my grandchildren for his Bible Bombers group, because his is the old metaphysics of endure this bad world and prepare for the next. As theologian Rosemary Ruether says, "The evaluation of mortal life as evil . . . has lent itself to an earth-fleeing ethic and spirituality, which has undoubtedly contributed very centrally to the neglect of the earth."[9]

I would have loved for my grandchildren to have sat with Joseph Mathews and to have listened to his new metaphysics of transparency, that life and creation are good and to be embraced as given, that Spirit dwells at the center of life, that Spirit can transform any situation by allowing us to see and to say *Yes* to the good creation: no mistake, a gift worthy of deepest thanksgiving.

What is going on spiritually in the universe is transparency: the transparency of matter, of time, of space, and of relationships. The universe in all its manifestations is constantly revealing Spirit, or as Teilhard de Chardin says, "The time has come for us to realize that to be satisfactory, any interpretation of the universe . . . must cover the inside as well as the outside of things — spirit as well as matter."[10] Everything has a spiritual as well as a material dimension. Teilhard, like few others in our time, has made us aware of the interior dimension of each element of the universe:

> Indisputably, deep within ourselves, through a rent or tear, an "interior" appears at the heart of beings. This is enough to establish the existence of this interior in some degree or other everywhere forever in nature . . . in every region of

time and space; . . . coextensive with its outside, everything has an inside. . . . Ultimately, somehow or other there must be only a single energy at play in the world.[11]

Elsewhere in his writings he says, "reality has become transparent," "in all things there is a *Within*," a "mysterious presence shining in the depths of things," "the heart of matter," "intimate depths," "the very heart of reality," and "depths of every event, every element."[12]

Tillich says it this way:

> [The] experience of the holy is mediated by some piece of finite reality. Everything can become a medium of revelation, a bearer of divine power. "Everything" not only includes all things in nature and culture, in soul and history; it also includes principles, categories, essences, and values.[13]

Everything can become a medium of revelation. Or everything is transparent to Spirit. What was not apparent suddenly shows through — is revealed. Martin Buber said it this way: "Every particular *Thou* is a glimpse through to the eternal *Thou*."[14] Or transparency happens: it is always an event of lesser or greater magnificence. Revealed transparently through any *event* and any *element* of creation, Spirit sustains and miraculously enlivens our consciousness and therefore our lives.

We all can list illustrations of transparency of matter, time, space, and relationships, to see how the universe shows its heart. One gazes at a flickering candle flame and encounters the transparent truth that light shines in darkness. One writes a memoir and sees the blessedness of the journey. One flies down the Shenandoah Valley and is overcome by the beauty of creation. One watches an ant colony do its work and sees through transparently to team effectiveness. One reads the Psalms and transparently becomes David railing at the Lord. One holds a new baby and encounters the transparent event of joy, always present but seldom experienced. One watches the movie *Judgment at Nuremberg* and sees clips of bulldozers pushing thousands of naked, gassed Jews into mass graves — or one sees the fireball of the planes hitting the World Trade Center — and experiences slaughter of the tribe and righteous rage. One sings a simple love song and discovers that s/he is singing it to all that is. One sees the African Children's Choir, who go transparent to all children in the third world who die in childhood from malnutrition or HIV/ AIDS. One looks at the Earthrise and sees home. One holds the hand of his dying mother and understands love.

In a real sense, all of this is looking at life and creation as Shakespeare knew: "All the world's a stage"; not only are we actors but we are also the audience, seeing what is going on, and sometimes — when transparency happens — what is *really* going on.

Art Form Methodology and Transparency

Consider the *art form* methodology.[15] One observes a work of art and discusses objective, reflective, and interpretive reactions to it, be it a movie, a painting, music, a poem, a play, literature. This method even allows one to meditate on life and contemplate creation. A three-way conversation takes place among *art form*, *creator*, and *oneself* as the viewer or listener.

Martin Heidegger saw that truth comes through the events of existence, *that what really is* gives itself to be known. This is also what he meant by "the clearing" (a phrase Ken Wilber uses; Mathews used "the center" in much the same way) in existence "within which Being presents itself": all ways to talk about transparency, or Spirit revealing Itself. When we see through to what really is in such a moment — beyond our willing and doing — we begin to see the depth dimension of reality.

The function of the *art form method* is to set us up to see through transparently and to name what we see as it really is: holy, full of wonder and mystery. Therefore, for me, the role of the artist is to make us aware of the awesomeness of life and creation. The use of the art form method — with its four levels: objective, reflective, interpretive, and indicative — is to help us focus on life in the earnest hope that we will be given to see what really is and participate with it.

This depth dynamic of human life and creation as a work of art — given to be seen through — is at the heart of what I mean by transparency, and likewise what I mean by the profound experience that religions have taken as their foundation. When transparency opens the clearing, or when we are given to see through to what really is, at the center, at the heart of creation, we have been encountered by Spirit. Teilhard says,

> [T]he whole of life lies in seeing — if not ultimately, at least essentially. . . . That is probably why the history of the living world can be reduced to the elaboration of ever more perfect eyes at the heart of the cosmos where it is always possible to discern more. . . . To try to see more and to see better is not . . . just a fantasy, curiosity, or a luxury. *See or perish*. This is the situation imposed on every element of the universe by the mysterious gift of existence.[16]

And so, for us humans, as one *element or species of the universe*, Spirit awakens us to see. Revelation happens to us when we are given the eyes to see what is potentially present in every situation and everything. When we really see what really is, we sometimes have an "aha" experience, and sometimes we spontaneously name something or someone as responsible: *YHWH*; *Abba*; the Holy; the Numinous. Or when this event happens, we may blurt out reverent expletives: my god; hallelujah; *wa* or *waduh* (Bahasa Indonesian words for "wow!" or "awesome!").

When transparency happens we understand eventfulness, newness, blind-but-now-I-see-ness. We understand what Moses understood seeing the burning bush on holy ground and why he hid his face: he could not look directly at the mysterious power of Spirit in the universe. We come to understand what awe is. We understand that we have been given to see Spirit that inspires, because It is incarnate in existence as It wilt, lo here and lo there, showing us Its presence transparently — as in Jacob's epiphany at Bethel — through the events of life in creation.

Being given to see transparently to the center of what is, within the stuff of life — in nothing special and in everything in particular — points to the understanding that each piece of creation is transparent to meaning, or just beneath the surface of each piece of external reality is meaning hiding in its interior reality. Or meaning is everywhere. Creation then becomes a sacred, wonder-full world.

This quote illustrates the point: "I used to think I was a perfectionist. I found the tiniest flaws in everything. Then I realized I was not a perfectionist at all; I was an imperfectionist! If I was a perfectionist, I would see perfection wherever I look."[17] If I see transparently, all is seen as good, perfect as is.

*****

To recapitulate, the mundane stuff-of-life event happens to us, revealing wonder and awe. In the moment of illumination we are given to see clearly what is. We feel compelled to interpret what is happening and name it. If the event opens us up in the deeps, we walk away knowing that we will not be the same. We internalize the happening, rehearsing it many times over. It leaves us with a depth resolve, either to call to remembrance, to bow in worship, to walk humbly with Spirit, to witness to Its power, to show compassion for creation — the comprehensive neighbor. When all this or any of this happens, we have experienced transparency.

During such transparent encounters, we go through some such process: focusing, reflecting, interpreting, internalizing, resolving, symbolizing, embodying, and serving. Or to use another scenario of the dynamics of transparency,

- an external event happens . . .
- which occasions an interior response . . .
- sometimes awaking us to the reality of the way life really is . . .
- and leaving us with the decision to elect or reject existence and creation — good as they are.

Transparency is the all-determining event for us humans. As Robert Frost wrote, let it happen over and over "till we answer from within," till we experience it, reflect upon it, interpret it, internalize it, embody it, and move out from the center of this event to live with new consciousness and sensitivity that will certainly alter our style of living. Spirit happens through everything that is, recreating and transforming what is in the eye of the beholder.

Spirit happens here and now, occasioning sight, and bringing us to sing with Louis

'What a wonderful world!'

Verse 12

heart of creation

from the heart of creation
whether it be
dinosaur or the latest e-

vent that invades consciousness
whether it be
a birth or catastrophe

Spirit is happening
whether it be
now or then in eternity

—*october 2001*

Verse 13

Here and Now

Not only do we live in the second-story
if we think that one day after we die we will go to another world,
or that we came from another world,
or that there is a something up there, out there, or back there
      that is finally in charge of life;
but also we live in the second-story
if we think there is Spirit out there
that we will one day grasp if we keep on the right path.
Second-story reality denies Spirit here and now,
denies that there is only one world of reality, and that this is it.

We are not preparing to live;
we are living now
at whatever age
or in whatever condition.
The kingdom is now, eternally.
Reality is present, here, at hand;
there is only one reality
and Spirit is its heart.

The life question is "What's happening?"
followed by "How do I fit in?"
Spirit shouts and whispers, "Let go! Follow Me!"
changing all It encounters.

Thus, to talk about Spirit, we talk about now,
not about the sweet-by-and-by of some ideal future,
when we finally enter a perfect state.

There is no two-, four-, six-, eight-step spirit journey.
There's just our recurring response to what's happening:
whether or not we give ourselves to Spirit's awesome lead.

Spirit is going on in our lives.
We can leap into It,
shut down and flat-line,
or do a lifelong search for It.
Two of the three are illusions.

Spirit is always already present,
erupting,
creating,
sanctifying,
whispering, "Here and Now!"
"Here and Now!"
ad infinitum.

—november 2000

Reflection 7

[A] *Spirit Comes as Wonder: Awesome, Gracious Eventfulness*

> [We] are dealing with something for which there is only one appropriate expression, "mysterium tremendum". The feeling of it may at times come sweeping like a gentle tide. . . . It may burst in sudden eruption up from the depths of the soul. . . . It may become the hushed, trembling, and speechless humility of the creature in the presence of — whom or what?
>
> [The element of fascination] may appear to the mind an object of horror and dread [other words for "awe"], but at the same time it is no less something that allures with a potent charm. . . . [I]t . . . bewilders and confounds. . . . [It comes as] the profound element of wonderfulness . . . "something more" . . . grace . . . blissful excitement, rapture, and exaltation . . . "like the resurrection of the dead" . . . [the] rapture of Nirvana .[1]   **~Rudolf Otto**

OTTO IS TALKING ABOUT an every-person encounter in life that has been here throughout the journey, one that no religion has a lock on but is the starting point for each. He is talking about a spirit experience that awes and even changes the human being. He took a couple of Kant's terms and came up with the word "numinous" and made it famous, to be used later by Jung and Teilhard de Chardin, especially. By "numinous," Otto meant grace, the holy, the sacred, which human consciousness is given to perceive in the very midst of life.

Numinous consciousness rattles and reshapes our perceptions of reality. We are set in life when we are radically opened up; we are pretty sure we have life figured out and in comes an event to expose our illusions; we had divided the world up into good and bad, black and white, first and last, and the dividing walls come tumbling down when we experience the awesome event; the bottom drops out of our reduced –isms and we see the oneness of all creation; we identify with Kierkegaard's Abraham, the exemplar of faith, for we too will always remember being transformed by the mystery's encounter. With him we come to understand that fear and trembling is the right relationship with the eternal event miraculously happening in our mundane lives.

The Secular, Every-person Event

Out of my tradition, I talk about such events as "grace." Paul Tillich says it best for me in his sermon "You Are Accepted," built upon his theology that Spirit, through moments of grace, is about revealing the truth to us who are blind through separation — all of us — until we experience and choose reunion:

> Sometimes at that moment a wave of light breaks into our darkness, and it is as though a voice were saying:
>
> "You are accepted. You are accepted, accepted by that which is greater than you, and the name of which you do not know. Do not ask for the name now; perhaps you will find it later. Do not do anything now; perhaps later you will do much. Do not seek for anything; do not perform anything; do not intend anything. *Simply accept the fact that you are accepted!*"

> If that happens to us, we experience grace. After such an experience we may not be better than before, and we may not believe more than before. But everything is transformed. . . . And nothing is demanded of this experience, no religious or moral or intellectual presuppositions, nothing but *acceptance*.[2]

This nonrational, secular spirit event happens "sometimes" to every person. This event comes as "a wave of light" or "a voice," and we feel ourselves at home. What does Tillich say the grace event does to our experience of "separation," "estrangement," or "alienation"? "In that moment, grace . . . bridges the gulf of estrangement."

The Spirit event of grace is the universal way we experience life, not dependent on any special religious understanding. It really is a nonreligious, secular event before it is interpreted as a religious event, and, therefore, this is what "in the beginning was the Word" means to me: there never has been a time when life was not this way. The religions picked up on the way life is and told their stories and created their creeds around the happenings of this secular event — grace being encountered in this world. Speaking across traditions, Tillich says we experience our sense of the separate-self as *at one* with what is: with the ground of being, with the other (all creation), and with oneself. One experiences grace reuniting all that is separated, making life whole.

Grace and Faith as Every-person Dynamics

Sometimes even our existential despair, our debilitating dread, our "sickness unto death" is transformed. We are given to see that we have become victims to the illusion that happiness is nowhere to be found, that the "ground of meaning" is forever lost. Sometimes, at such moments, grace happens and reveals to us our rejection of life as it is — we are telling ourselves life is bad, not fair, worthless. Such rejection is the essence of our despair. Paradoxically grace reveals to us at such moments that life and our lives as they are, are good, regardless of what we think or feel. Life, Spirit, grace — whichever word you like — accepts us as the despairing ones we are, giving us the possibility to see life as it really is, as good, with the possibility to elect to have our real lives. This fundamental decision my tradition calls "faith" — which comes in the encounter with grace or the *Yes* of Spirit — our saying *Yes* in return, or as Tillich says, *accepting* "the fact that you are accepted."[3]

For me, *grace gives the possibility to decide; faith is to decide*, to accept our acceptance (not by grace alone [direct union] or faith alone [union by our initiative — works], but by grace-through-faith). Does the Spirit encounter us? Of course. Does It depend upon us? Yes. We have a decision to make when encountered: *Yes* or *No*. Some say, "I am what God makes me." I say, I am who I choose to be as I live in the event or memory of grace. When I decide to "accept the fact that I am accepted," transformation is the result: my identity is no longer the separated self but the reunited self. I am healed, if you will, during moments of grace.

Does despair go away? Yes, for a while. Does it reign over our lives as before? No, not if we accept the fact that we are accepted, or if we remember the glory and peace of reunion. At least we become victorious despairing ones, living and dying with a smile in our being, like Lord Buddha, for we know that life is good, or as the Mormon hymn says, "All is well. All is well." We have been given to know the supreme secret of existence.

Personal Examples of the Awesome Event

Once I was sitting in my room in the West Side ghetto of Chicago, in despair over my lack of effectiveness in helping the African-

American community leaders work through a crucial decision that affected the future of the community. Of course I was blaming them. Deep dialogue was erupting in me: They don't care. This situation is hopeless. What am I doing here, anyway? Where can I go if I leave? What a failure I am.

I asked a friend for help. All he said was, "Have you ever read Tillich's *The Courage To Be?*" I borrowed it from him and read most of it the same night. The word I needed to hear came through: courage to accept one's acceptance is the same as the courage to accept one's despair. "The act of accepting meaninglessness is in itself a meaningful act. It is an act of faith."[4] I was being driven to despair, which was driving me to faith, to the courage to be who I really was at that moment: a despairing, defeated young man. That was the first time I ever really heard that despair was good, even redemptive. Tears washed my being. I experienced a wave of peace, and the word "All is well, John," got said to me powerfully. From somewhere I heard the all-important fact of life that I was accepted in the condition I was in — despair — and I said *Yes*, breathed deeply, laid the book down, and fell asleep.

Did I go out and conquer the situation the next day. Not exactly, but I did have a new appreciation for the leaders, a new perspective on the situation, and there for a while I was more effective in relating to most everything around me. The leader of the community told me I seemed to be different, easier to work with. I can't remember how they dealt with the community issue, but I do remember that personally transforming event to this day, some thirty years later, and rehearse again the way life is and the way Spirit operates in everyday, secular existence.

Another way to test Spirit, according to Tillich, is also contained in my personal illustration:

> If the divine Spirit breaks into the human spirit, this does not mean that it rests there, but that it drives the human

> spirit out of itself. . . . The [human] spirit, a dimension
> of finite life, is driven into a successful self-
> transcendence; it is grasped by something ultimate and
> unconditional. It is still human spirit; it remains what
> it is, but at the same time, it goes out of itself under the
> impact of the divine Spirit.[5]

I was freed up to go back into the situation. I could have quit and left. Upon reflection, I went *out of myself*, was empowered to transcend myself, under the impact of the Spirit in my despair.

Spirit comes in myriad ways, as Otto's quote says at the beginning: "sudden eruption up from the depths of the soul"; "sweeping like a gentle tide"; "hushed, trembling, and speechless humility of the creature in the presence of — whom or what"; "horror and dread"; "allures with a potent charm"; "bewilders and confounds"; "the profound element of *wonderfulness*"; "'something more'"; "grace"; "blissful excitement, rapture, and exaltation"; "'like the resurrection of the dead'"; "rapture of Nirvana."

It has come to me in big and small ways when I was

- a boy taking Christmas baskets to "Colored Hill" with my father
- falling in love with Lynda
- holding a new baby, especially sons John and Jeremiah and my two grandchildren
- learning of the assassination of JFK
- totaling my red VW Bug on I-94 and barely escaping death
- a college student listening to the majestic "Prologue" to Boïto's *Mefistofele*
- working with a ghetto (and a village) that picked up its life
- reading *Grace and Grit* by Ken Wilber
- attending the spirit-filled memorial service of my mentor
- hearing that the life of our close friends' son tragically ended in suicide
- experiencing the tragedy of September 11

Mysterious Spirit and the Other World in This World

Mysterious Spirit encounters us in this life, in this world. Ancient Greek philosophy and many today act as though Spirit is otherworldly. I am much more Jew than Greek. In fact, I like to say I am Judaic-Christian by tradition. Both were clear that creation was holy because of the presence of Spirit. Creation is where Spirit happens. Spirit is in creation's history from beginning to end, sanctifying it. Our lives are good because Spirit is everlastingly here through Its encounters. I have never seen Spirit anything, but I keep experiencing It.

Spirit has many names and many ways of *eventing* us. It is here, awesome, and full of grace. Furthermore, my experience tells me It is on our side and that It is the only thing we can finally trust.

The Other World Charts name this first arena we have been describing as "The Land of Mystery," all about wonder and humility. It is divided into four subsections or treks:

> *Trek I*: Impacted by mystery — awe-full encounter:
>   primordial wonder
> *Trek II*: Enveloped by mystery — inescapable power:
>   final limits
> *Trek III*: Recreated by mystery — transformed state:
>   all things are new
> *Trek IV*: Seduced by mystery — infinite passion:
>   adoration of being

And under these four treks are sixteen states of being that every person experiences, more or less, from womb to tomb.

What is the mysterious Spirit out to do? Bring us to the adoration of being in creation, life, and our lives. Through Its encounter, we experience a *big feel*, a *big think*, and a *big resolve*,

as Mathews liked to say. Spirit is the deepest thing we experience.
Swiss psychiatrist C. G. Jung said,

> The main interest of my work is not concerned with the
> treatment of neurosis but rather with the approach to the
> numinous . . . [which] is the real therapy and inasmuch as
> you attain to the numinous experiences you are released
> from the curse of pathology.[6]

Again, as Mathews said in Reflection 6, "The poetry . . .
[and the] new mythology [of the other world in this world will]
enable us to find our way to swim [and not drown], if you please,
in the rivers of radical consciousness and become human."
The Land of Mystery is all about

• how we experience wonder and awe
• how we relate to the numinous Spirit as It encounters us day by day
• how we sometimes experience Its acceptance of us just as we are
• how we simply accept the fact that we are acceptable and accepted
• how we know above all else that "all is well"
• and how we respond to Its leading.

Spirit comes as mystery — awesome, gracious eventfulness —
that transforms life.

Verse 14   *Epiphany*

creation's
Spirit heart
is beating

Spirit's good
all is good
life is good

Spirit's no-
where if not
everywhere

celebrate
"Spirit's here!"
this season

—january 2001

Verse 15   *Eternal Now*

what is
reveals itself now
continually
for me
to see

i see
with open eyes and
one big joyful heart
grateful
to be

—january 2001

123

Reflection 8

[B] *Spirit Comes as Freedom:*
A Conscious Rhapsody of Choice

> The *Thou* confronts me. But I step into direct relation
> with it. Hence the relation means being chosen and choos-
> ing. . . . Going out to the relation cannot be taught. . . .
> [A]ll the preparations, exercises, and meditations . . .
> have nothing to do with the primally simple fact of en-
> counter. . . . [T]he one thing needful becomes visible:
> the total acceptance of the present. . . . What has to be
> given up is not the I, as most mystics suppose: the I is
> indispensable for any relationship, including the highest
> . . . between *I* and *Thou*.[1]   **~Martin Buber**

BUBER'S QUOTE CONNECTS the Land of Mystery, the first
dynamic of Spirit in Reflection 7, to the second dynamic in this
Reflection, the River of Consciousness. In the meeting or
encounter with Spirit, we find our true identity: *the free self
becomes aware of being chosen and choosing* — without either,
Spirit or self, there is no real meeting or real meaning in life. In
the first dynamic of spirit, the emphasis is on the happening or
event of Spirit. In this Reflection the emphasis is on our freedom
of choice in response to Spirit happening in our lives.

    The Other World Charts[2] depict four arenas of human
consciousness, but Joseph Mathews reminds us,

> Actually, in the Other World [in This World] there is only
> one state of being, not four. For where *consciousness* is,

there is the *mystery*, there is the world on your back [*care*], and there is the peace [*tranquility*] that passes reason's capacity to grasp it.[3]

A primary function of consciousness is to connect us to Spirit.

Kierkegaard and Buber on Freedom

Søren Kierkegaard suggests that this second dynamic is about consciously being at one with that which constitutes life, or saying *Yes* to life as given, or leaping into life. He has made it clearer than most in the last hundred and fifty years that Spirit is not real to anyone without the "leap into eternity," which suggests leaping into the unknown and into uncertainty with passionate faith — risking the possibility of being in error as well as in truth, and in the leap being united with that which "posits" us. What does this mean? What is it like?

The leap is not unlike a small boy, who cannot swim, jumping for the first time into the arms of his father waiting in the deep water; or not unlike one's making a first jump into the outstretched hands of a swinging trapeze catcher; or not unlike one's jumping from a third-story window into a stretched canvas, held by firemen and neighbors, to escape the raging fire. In these examples one is jumping toward something she trusts will receive her safely or will not let her come to harm.

Nevertheless, the leap is always experienced as a risk, sometimes out "over seventy thousand fathoms of water,"[4] demanding one to struggle to decide in the midst of fear and trembling to do or not to do what one decides is right. Our courage to decide is rooted in the freedom born of possibility — that according to Kierkegaard "never disappoints" — at the center of life and our lives. Or as Jose Ortega y Gasset wrote, "Living is a constant process of deciding what we are going to do." One can observe, judge, and weigh up over and over but finally must decide and leap. There is no authentic relationship to Spirit without decision and action, "the leap of faith," according to Kierkegaard. In a real sense, one becomes at one with Spirit as one trusts It with one's life. This is grounding life in actuality rather than in some theory or doctrine that usually requires no risk. The leap is born of one's awesome consciousness of freedom and is the awesome act of freedom begun in choice.

As in Buber's quote at the beginning of the Reflection, the authentic relationship calls forth an act of the self, not a belief in some spirit that saves without one's free act of choice. Both Buber and Kierkegaard are saying that Spirit is out to change our lives by calling us to choose to be our true selves in life's decisive encounters. Therefore, in the response to meeting Spirit, the self (the *I*) is actualized. Buber believed that every life event was an event in which Spirit (Eternal *Thou*) addresses us, and we are called to answer through decision.

> Everything on our way involves decision — intentional, dimly sensed, or wholly secret: but this in the innermost being is the primal mysterious decision, carrying the mightiest consequences for our destiny.[5]

The Order: Ecumenical built its understanding of "consciousness of consciousness of consciousness" on Kierkegaard's formula of the self in relation to Spirit (he used the word "Power").

> by relating itself to its own self and by willing to be itself the self is grounded transparently in the Power which posited [constituted] it.[6]

This is "grounding" the self in real life. Here Kierkegaard says the Spirit helps us to become our true selves. Faith in the Spirit is the choice to be the self one is. In response to the encounter of Spirit the self is actualized.

Another way to look at Kierkegaard's Spirit formula is to consider it as the process of consciousness. I cannot choose to be a self other than the one I actually am, and that self is a self usually in "disrelationship" — Kierkegaard's word for "despair" or "sin." If I hear the call to live who I really am, I am given the choice to leap into or seize possibility. If I do, at that moment I experience life as it truly is. "By relating itself to its own self (first consciousness) and by willing to be itself (second consciousness), the self is grounded transparently in the Power (third consciousness) which posited it."

Examples of Kierkegaard's Spirit Formula

Some examples of Kierkegaard's formula follow. The Order: Ecumenical and the Ecumenical Institute read Kierkegaard's formula of consciousness this way: we know Spirit is happening to us when

1. an *external event*
2. occasions an *internal crisis*
3. calling forth a *life-question* (whether to elect or reject our life-situation)
4. from which we wish to *escape*, most often.

Spirit is real for us when these dynamics are happening. My colleague Gene Marshall adds, "If we choose *not to escape*, then Spirit is manifest in our lives in its healthy form."[7]

Einstein's equation experience is an example:

1. *external event*

> in a Berlin apartment sitting at his desk on November 22, 1914, Einstein looked at his formulas scratched on a white piece of paper and

became aware that the universe is ever expanding in every direction infinitely

2. *internal crisis*

Einstein struggled to believe the whole truth of his equations, which flew in the face of three-hundred years of Newtonian "truth," and therefore was most reluctant to share them with the scientific community

3. *life-question*

will I share this unbelievable revelation for the sake of the future but thereby risk my future professionally

4. *escape*

Einstein lost his nerve and doctored his equations, trying to have it both ways (only later, when Hubble invited him to look through the telescope at Mt. Palomar in the 1920's, did Einstein confirm the undeniable truth of the initial equations)[8]

Maybe this example of Einstein seems abstract to most of us who are not geniuses. Let us try a more every-person example, addiction:

1. *external event*

in a finger-pointing accusation, my friend's wife called him a drunk

2. *internal crisis*

he slapped her; she left him and filed for divorce; he was devastated by his own brutality in the face of the awful "truth"

3. *life-question*

am I really a drunk, and if so, will I continue to deny it or get help

4. *escape*

> my friend went on the biggest binge of his life (later, he sought professional help and reunited with his wife; his life was transformed because of the truth)

A last example of the spirit formula applies to everyone, since we all will die:

1. *external event*

> my young friend, a mother of three, was told she had cancer and had a short time to live

2. *internal crisis*

> deep grief resulted in private with her husband, children, and extended family

3. *life-question*

> will I die before I die or will I live my dying to the hilt on behalf of those I love

4. *not escape*

> she became a powerful role-model of celebrating life until her death; she realized a dream to establish a foundation for children; her memorial service overflowed with friends; Spirit was definitely manifested through her in a healthy form as she said *Yes* to living and dying

At its simplest, something significant happens that makes us conscious in a new way; we take a new relationship; and we experience a deep relationship with life as it really is. If this happens to us, we have come in touch with Spirit. We can understand the events of our lives as blessings, accidents, curses, or punishments. Why not say that the events that bring us to depth consciousness are not a problem but an opportunity to take a creative relationship to them and by so doing be related to Spirit, which is our ground of meaning?

In sum, consciousness is not the same as Spirit, but the process of consciousness, as Kierkegaard might have said, is the primary way all humans experience the encounter with Spirit. Or as Buber might have said, in the meeting with Spirit we find our true identity: *the free self becomes aware of being chosen and choosing.* Without the Spirit event and without the free *Yes* of the self in response to It, there is no genuine meeting.

In life we are always being given a free decision, transparently, for or against truth or the way life is — and our life is — constituted. We can affirm the way life is or negate it: *Yes* or *No.* And if life is — and our lives are — good as created, then we are sometimes reunited in our decisions with the goodness of life as given, constituted, or posited.

From our side, the key to all this is the exercise of our freedom, our choice to say *Yes* in the crisis of decision. It's a choice because we can also say *No*, and more often do, missing out on the healing and renewing power in life.

In the first dynamic (wonder or mystery) of Spirit in the last Reflection, the emphasis is on the happening of Spirit. Here the emphasis is on our freedom of choice in response to the happening of Spirit in our lives. This second dynamic of Spirit — conscious freedom — is referred to in *The Other World Charts* as

> *Trek V*: Freedom of awareness — authentic relationship:
>   I am my consciousness
> *Trek VI*: Freedom of inventiveness — creative existence:
>   I am my originality
> *Trek VII*: Freedom of decision — moral ground:
>   I am my conscience
> *Trek VIII*: Freedom of obligation — final accountability:
>   I am my answerability

Depth Existentialism

We have been using Kierkegaard and Buber's definition of Spirit in relation to the self of the human. *Depth existentialism* starts here. Many there are who say existentialism in its concern for the self and redemption of the individual is a reduction of the activity of Spirit.

> The existentialist dichotomy between the sphere of personal selfhood and the sphere of impersonal objects can also be criticized on theological and ethical grounds. The retreat to the realm of human inwardness leaves nature unrelated to God and devoid of enduring significance. What was God doing in the long history of the cosmos before the appearance of humanity? Is the world only the impersonal stage for the drama of human life? Should we then treat it as an object to be exploited for human benefit?[9]   **~Ian Barbour**

I would agree if the spirit dynamics in relation to the human stopped there. But they don't. This reflection has been talking about the personal, responding self of the human. We have emphasized the act before the act, as it were, the *free choice*. But Spirit, eternally creating and redeeming the society and the cosmos as well as the individual, acts in history and nature, time and space. In the next reflection we will emphasize the *free deed* on behalf of all creation that comes out of the *free choice*.

One has to say that Spirit does not *just* happen in the human domain. Yet, we have to admit that Spirit does happen there, through the freedom of our choosing to be.

In Sum

Spirit's gift of freedom comes to us as a conscious rhapsody of being chosen and choosing. Freedom's dynamics are held in the verse of this song:

> Free am I, now beyond good and evil,
> Deciding the right and surrend'ring the deed.
> Ever smiled upon by the mercy of Being,
> I'm then commissioned endlessly.[10]

Or again in this song, written in the 60s by the Ecumenical Institute: Chicago, called "Responsibility," from the insights of Dietrich Bonhoeffer in his *Ethics* and sung to the Beattles' tune *Yellow Submarine* (quite a combination, Bonhoeffer and the Beattles):

> *Refrain*:
> Free men live in responsibility, duty bound and free, in relativity;
> Free men live in responsibility, whoever they may be,
>> their deeds are history.

Observe and judge the given facts, weigh up the values, decide and act.
You're alone, completely free, leave the judgment to history.

To no principle, no law, to no authority can you withdraw.
You decide it all alone, right from right and wrong from wrong.

Obligation is the call, to God and neighbor surrender all.
The free venture is the deed, rendered up to meet the need.[11]

We are journeyed through life by mysterious Spirit that will not let us be till we grasp our freedom, with fear and fascination, till we say *Yes* or *No*. This is the glory of being human. How do we know Spirit is real? Experiencing being chosen to decide, and deciding, again and again, endlessly, and on behalf of: this is the conscious rhapsody of our lives.

Meeting

if the meeting is the thing
between Spirit and me
I'm glad we are two
with eventful dialogue

if we were one
we couldn't meet
so I promise to be
on time and present

'cause maybe it's me
missing the meetings
if Spirit's always present
and never once late

a big meeting past
when assassinations
flipped my universe
and my life's direction

or a little meeting today
when granddaughter
penned 'I LOV YU'
for her first sentence

I'll look and listen
through such events

for the meeting next
between thou and me

for these meetings
illumine my life
making the mundane
holy comm-union

"let's continue to meet
on the sly or
in broad daylight
again and every now"

—*september 2001*

Meaning

more stuff gives meaning
entertainment gives meaning
long life gives meaning

they say
no

they say
thanksgiving for life the way it is gives meaning
giving life where it isn't gives meaning

they say
you don't have to go to school to find meaning
you don't have to be rich to find meaning

they say
the meaning of life is to expend it
expend it before the age of 33 and after

they say
you mess up
trying to save it

who are they anyway
and how'd they figure what to say

—*october 2000*

Reflection 9

[C] *Spirit Comes as Care: Wondrous Deeds*

> ... Thank God our time is now, when wrong
> Comes up to face us everywhere,
> Never to leave us till we take
> The longest stride of soul men ever took.
> Affairs are now soul size.[1]
>   **~Christopher Fry**

FRY WAS WRITING WHEN the murder of six million Jews was still fresh in mind, when over 90 percent of the Jews of Lithuania were slaughtered, when nearly 200,000 Japanese were wiped out in Hiroshima and Nagasaki by the first atomic bombs.

If he were writing it today, other atrocities would be fresh in mind: the HIV/AIDS pandemic, 24,000 deaths each day from hunger, racial cleansing in Ruwanda and Bosnia, 23,000 species wiped out each year never to return, global warming caused especially by the increased auto emissions during the last decades, international trafficking in humans for sweat shops and prostitution, drug trafficking, accelerating global poverty, and the terrorist attacks on September 11. Everyone can add to the list. "[W]rong/ Comes up to face us everywhere, /Never to leave us till we take/ The longest stride of soul men ever took." Crisis calls. Care is our response. Spirit makes Itself known in crisis and care.

137

The Experience Within the Experience of September 11

What was really going on during and after the events of
September 11? What was really happening to us? What was my
deep, personal experience?

Taking Rudolf Otto's ontology and Edmund Husserl's
phenomenology seriously, the Order and the Institutes described
such an experience this way: an external event of awe happens
that sets off an event within the event, which is experienced as a
big feel, *big think*, and *big resolve* — this interior experience can
be called a "state of being." In short, an awesome event grabs our
consciousness, sometimes shakes our foundations, and allows us
to see transparently the deep meaning of life.

As alluded to in Reflections 6 and 7, awe is a sure sign
of Spirit in our lives. Awe, as Otto says, is often palpable and
even frightening, leaving us with dread as well as fascination.
In the awesome events around 9/11, dread and radical insecurity
were the collective experience. Global humanity surely
experienced awe. We experienced awe through external events:
the plane attacks on the buildings overwhelmed us in the events
we called "surreal."

Overwhelmed, we could not think straight or resolve much
of anything at first, but we experienced the *big feel* like few times
in our lives: we described our feelings as universal shock, grief,
numbness, paralysis, rage, heartfelt compassion. Prose was hardly
adequate, so we started writing poetry, trying to articulate our
depth experience of feeling.

We had to do something! We first resolved to care for the
victims with a mighty global outpouring of vigils, charity, and
volunteerism. This resolve grew into a *big resolve* of war by
some, peace by others, justice by most, focused on fighting global
terrorism and rooting out its global causes.

This resolve was intertwining with the *big think*: Why
would anybody do such a thing intentionally? Unfathomable. Why

are we so divided globally? How is it possible that our religions are motivating such action, as the terrorists proclaim? What is Islam all about? Why is "globalization" such a dirty word, and why are transnational corporations and their public relations firms being indicted? Why are there so many poor people on the Earth when there are such pockets of abundance in every nation, and especially in the West and in Arab fiefdoms such as Saudi Arabia? How did things get so out of balance? "History is born out of a sudden imbalance which fissures society at every level." I think Sartre's quote is for this time of rupture in our personal, national, and international systems. As Fry says, it's time to "take the longest stride of soul" we've ever taken. Spirit is changing us through these events.

To move from general reactions, let me share my personal experience of this national and global experience of September 11.

- *My "big feel"*: after being awestruck by the falling towers, the clouds of ash, the horror stories of people leaping hand in hand, hundreds of people trying to rescue victims and becoming victims themselves, people running in the streets, the reports of last-minute phone calls, people in shock being interviewed, people in helpless grief looking for their relatives and mates, the seemingly eternal flame and smoke from ground zero, and the ceaseless repetition of the images of the balls of fire on TV, I collapsed into a heap of despair and sorrow, with fits of rage at the fanatics that perpetrated the events and the warmongering rhetoric from a seeming majority of my fellow Americans; I understood but was enraged by their eye-for-an-eye response. The best way I can now recollect my state of being then, after those first few hours, was a *consuming doom: there is no way out of this nightmare.*

- *My "big think"*: the most immediate reflective thought I had was *this world, our world, my world will never be the same*, for our illusions of security were dashed in terrorism that can never be finally controlled, much less stopped. The events of 9/11 swept illusions away. I experienced a new reality at hand, revolutionizing our lives. This new reality has a flag with the big blue marble on it, blowing in the wind, and one of its new theme songs goes, "God bless the planet Earth/ Land that we love." No longer can we just say "God Bless America."

- *My "big resolve"*: what reverberated deepest was an *unliftable burden of care for the world.* How can we deal with this? How will we come together? Who will lead the way? How can our resolve ever match the resolve of the terrorists? But I was at least facing future's direction: I knew I really cared for the planet. I realized that unless we cared for all our provincial cares for our own and ourselves were unrealizable fantasies of a bygone day, gone forever. I remembered Juan Luis Segundo's quote, "The thrust of man's proper balance in the future is placing the fate of all in the hands of all." Then came the question, What are you going to do about all this, John? My new resolve after 9/11 was to finish this book that might help us to see that we are on one planetary spirit journey, which is the hope for Earth's reconciliation and restoration.

In the midst of deeply experiencing this experience of September 11, there was a strange new power rising in me, from a new gift of perception, from a new gift of communion with the tribe, from a new gift of motivation to care for my Earth. I was transformed, at least for a short time, by the spirit event of September 11, and I know that the memory of that encounter will not let me go but will revisit me for the rest of my life. That's the way Spirit works.

A Mountain of Care

Spirit has turned the world into a mountain of care and Spirit calls us to care for that mountain. Care is the third dynamic of Spirit on *The Other World Charts*. Through our care, Spirit releases soul-service to the world. The following treks describe such care:

> *Trek IX*: Original gratitude — care is appreciation:
>   sacramental universe
> *Trek X*: Universal concern — care is compassion:
>   binding wounds of time
> *Trek XI*: Singular mission — care is responsibility for:
>   everything is my kin
> *Trek XII*: Transparent power — care is motivity:
>   moving mountains

The "sacramental universe" of Trek IX is conceptualized well by Kazantzakis:

> Suddenly I know that my whole life hangs on this decision — the life of the entire Universe.[2]

> Everything you do reverberates throughout a thousand destinies.[3]

Our destiny is on behalf of the past, present, and future, to care for creation on this blue ball called Earth.

Our Mission of Care

What is our destinal role as humans? We get clues from what we have done in the past. Since the writing of a human Bill of Rights in the USA, we human citizens of the globe have been about ending slavery; outlawing child labor; championing women's rights; organizing labor negotiations; defeating Nazism, Fascism, and dictatorships; implementing the Marshall Plan in Europe and a similar plan in Japan; convening the United Nations; ending colonialism through such efforts as Gandhi's nonviolent movement in India. Out of that movement came the nonviolent civil rights movement in the USA; the nonviolent protest of Communism in Poland; the nonviolent protests against the bad war decision of Viet Nam. Later came the fall of the Berlin Wall and the end of the cold war and the USSR. Then we wrote the Earth Charter and the Universe Story. We reconvened the Parliament of the World's Religions, formally ended apartheid through instruments such as the Truth and Reconciliation Commission. We organized global crime tribunals, a global coalition to fight terrorism, and a global plan to restore Afghanistan.

Inversely, what we have not done, or been blocked in doing, gives us clues as to our destinal human role. A set of key words makes it plain: poverty; HIV/AIDS; drugs; population; global warming; petroleum dependence; water shortage; species extinction; rain forests depletion; excessive incarcerations; Israel/ Palestine; Iraq; Kashmir; global fanaticism; oppressive governments and fiefdoms; and the new colonialism of transnational corporations. Underlying all these is a gasping value system. We have climbed only to the lower heights of our planetary mountain of care.

Whence Wondrous Deeds?

We have read enough history and lived long enough to know that the next big climb up the mountain of care will *not* come with better technology, better Genome experimentation, better national GNPs, better governmental programs, more jobs and better salaries, or even with better education.

To climb further up the mountain we must address the global value system as we globally reflect on our great accomplishments over the more than two-hundred years since the human Bill of Rights in the USA.

We are left with the question of what brought forth Jefferson, Lincoln, Sojourner Truth, Rauschenbusch, Einstein, Teilhard de Chardin, Gandhi, Churchill, Franklin Roosevelt, George Marshall, Rosa Parks, Martin Luther King, Jr., Rachel Carson, John Kennedy, Dag Hammarskjöld, Lech Walesa, Thich Nhat Hanh, Nelson Mandela, Thomas Berry, Desmond Tutu, Wangari Maathai, Vandana Shiva, and all the rest?

These heroes had/have a different set of values. They had soul-training for the "soul-sized affairs" of their time. Amazingly, they gave form to freedom, nonviolence, a forgiveness commission, care for refugees, the new universe story, human sacrifice, universe science, transformative literature, and massive social reconstruction. Where did such values come from? Out of deep encounters with Spirit with Its biggest questions during "dark and cold winters" of the long journey. Their values were forged in depth spirit formation that makes them ready when called to be servants, to bind the wounds of time, and to create new ways for all the Earth. They understood/understand there is no such thing as spirituality without sacrifice.

Later we will explore some of their profound journey preparation and reflect on the same for us and our day, but it is enough to say here that they were trained to be spirit leaders and responded when moved by the Spirit. Their free *Yes* decisions and *wondrous deeds* have set the high water mark for our generation of planetary servants, to whom much is given and from whom much is demanded.

> Our deepest fear is not that we are inadequate
> Our deepest fear is that we are powerful beyond measure;
> It is our light, not our darkness, that frightens us. . . .
> Your playing small doesn't serve the world. . . .

And as we let our own light shine,
We unconsciously give other people permission to do the same.
As we are liberated from our fears,
Our presence automatically liberates others.

These lines from Nelson Mandela's inauguration speech of 1994
tell us that our transparent power in the Spirit is what cares for
the mountain, what helps transform creation. If it takes twenty-
seven years in Robben Island Prison to forge that power, so be it.
The Spirit often uses such severe means to move such mountains
as apartheid. As our scriptures say, Spirit will give us power to
move mountains, telling this mountain to pick up and move over
there. We were born to move mountains and in so doing renew
the Earth. Old religious poetry says it this way:

> When you send forth your spirit [*ruah YHVH*[4]],
>   they are created,
> and you give new life to the earth.
> **~Psalms** 104: 30

Out of that tradition, Buber says it this way: the human "feels and
comprehends the enthusiasm which overwhelms him, the
overpowering working within him of the spirit. . . ."[5] *Spirit is
the "whence" of wondrous deeds.*

The song "Spirit of Care"[6] borrows poetry from *The Other World
Charts* and reminds us where we are coming from:

> No one to hate
> Cleanly restored
> Finally moving as one spirit
>   dancing through doors
> Surrounded by harmony
>   echoing two million songs
> Earthrise alive
>   New age belongs

Hope beyond hope
Sacred intent
Ceaselessly suffering
Never relent
People who care
Spirit of care
        Triumphantly won

Carried by waves
Lives ever claimed
No-thing compels us to love
Always unnamed
People who care
Spirit of care
        Eternally one

Verse 18

Happy Birthday, Thomas

Billions of years ago
more or less
you began with a bang
and ever since
you've been evolving

You've had a home
on Earth
in the universe
with one humongous family
of kindred spirits
from butterflies to Teilhard
brothers and sisters all

You've been sustained
even loved
by what has been
is now
and is ever coming

Think about
the next phase
of your journey
in peace
flow like the river
toward the tranquil sea
and crashing waves

Fear not
lest you be forgotten
for you have been
are and will always be
a blessed member
of this intercommunion

That keeps creating
transforming
eternally
that has no place to go
save Spirit is
already there

—*for Thomas Berry's birthday*
november 9, 2001

Reflection 10

[D] *Spirit Comes as Fulfillment:*
The Happy Life

There is a strange consuming happiness in acting with the full knowledge that whatever one is doing may very well be one's last act on earth.[1]   ~Carlos Castaneda

Life is good and death is good.[2]

What is meant by happiness? To live every unhappiness.[3]
                                        ~Nikos Kazantzakis

I like the way Dylan Thomas put it when he said, "After the first death, there is no other." . . . Death is a part of my life. My life is a part of my life. My life, then, is my life and my death. Or let me put it this way: my life is always my life embracing my death. . . . And that's a constant process. . . . In such embracing I have life. I am alive. . . . In uttering *Yes* to my relationship [with life and death], at that moment, I have eternal life. My being is not what happens to me, including my not breathing ever again. My being is a transformed spirit that comes by virtue of the *Yes*. . . .[4]   ~Joseph A. Slicker

I'M NOT SURE ANYONE CAN COMMUNICATE the meaning of fulfillment, tranquility, peace, endlessness, eternal life. Yet, as I have gone around the world asking such questions as What have been moments of fulfillment for you?

149

and When have you been fulfilled? the answers are remarkably the same: when I held my first baby, when I was fully engaged in helping some being or community of beings, when I realized a lifetime dream, when I was with my family at a special celebration. It makes no difference whether I raise such questions with poor villagers in India or residents of a ghetto in Chicago, with well-off suburbanites or with children or elders, with people of faith or with secular types, the answers are very similar. I have been surprised that they seldom use religious words, and everyone could go on and on recounting moments in their lives when they were fulfilled. Fulfillment is obviously a universal experience.

Living in the 21st century as an aspiring Ecozoic man, I know of no other world out there beyond this world. I experience being inside my experience looking out. All I know is that I experience the other world in the midst of living in this world. I experience awe. I experience having a profound conversation with *that* which catalyzes my deep consciousness, and we go round and round conversing about what triggered my experience and my reaction to it, trying to really understand what happened and is now happening.

When that sort of interior dialogue is initiated by an encounter with Spirit, we find ourselves in a state of being in the other world, where we almost transcend living and dying, at least momentarily. I experience myself visiting the other world, or I am keenly aware of the profound in the mundane. I experience myself looking at myself from outside myself, realizing I am, that I am in being. All this is not ethereal, mystical, otherworldly, but human in our stages of consciousness as we experience Spirit, or in our states of being as we experience Spirit's presence.

The Kingdom Come

What is the state of being of final fulfillment, endlessness, blessed peace, eternal bliss, magnanimous tranquility? How is it we experience such profound states of consciousness? What difference do they make in our lives?

The answers come back during hard-to-articulate kairotic moments in life when "time stands still" or when "time is cut in two." "Time is the Life of the soul," Longfellow wrote; let me add: of the soul *in response to Spirit.* There would not be chronological time unless we humans in our consciousness had not been encountered over and over again by kairotic moments. Time is even created by memorable, kairotic moments when Spirit makes Itself known in our existence and therefore marks it. Had there not been spirit exclamations, maybe there would not be mundane commas ticking off chronological time. In my life history there was Pearl Harbor and 9/11/2001 that constituted what was before and after, creating memorable marks for my lifetime.

Sam Keen describes kairotic time:

> The realm of the spirit operates on kairotic rather than chronological time. Nothing graceful happens by the numbers. . . . Great and soulful events — falling in love, openings to the Beyond-Within, the birth of ideas and babies — march to no tick-tock but appear in their own good time, when the heart is prepared and the moment is ripe.[5]

Jim Marion writes about the "Kingdom of Heaven" in this kairotic context:

> the Kingdom of Heaven was something that could be realized by each and every one of us right here on Earth. It was a Kingdom that could actually be "seen," not with our physical eyes, of course, but with the inner eye of understanding. The goal of the spiritual life, Jesus taught, was to "seek first" this inner vision of this world. . . . The goal of Christian spirituality, the spirituality that Jesus himself preached, is for each and every one of us to personally be able to see the Kingdom of Heaven within, that Jesus saw.[6]

Fulfillment comes not at the end of life but throughout life. Heaven is in the midst of life. Eternal life or endlessness are in the midst of life. This truth is the heart of the spiritual revolution this book is describing: our universal spirit tradition is all about experiencing the full life here and now, not there and then. Therefore, the kairotic, eternal moment of Spirit's presence manifests the promise of fulfilled life, here and now.

Final Fulfillment

We talked about final fulfillment in Reflection 7 as knowing all is well in the great event of grace that makes life whole and new. This is finally all we need to know, that life as it is, and our lives as they are, are fulfilled in the experiences

- that life is good as created
- that we are accepted as we are
- that our past is approved, and
- that our future is utterly possible.

There are many ways to articulate this truth and the great religions have been about that task. However ultimate truth comes, we know all we need to know to live the fulfilled life. The search ends here. Why go looking for any more truth than this ultimate truth that we have already experienced? Foolish! Once the secret of life has been found, stop looking. "[Y]ou never find happiness until you stop looking for it," says Chuang Tzu.[7] I think the experience of fulfillment or happiness is what he is talking about.

Curly, in the movie *City Slickers*, says it this way to those city slickers who went west in search of the truth about life:

> **Curly** (Jack Palance): Do you know what the secret of life is? One thing [holds up index finger of his right hand with authority]. Just one thing. You stick to that and every

thing else don't mean shit.
Mitch (Billy Crystal): Yeah, but what's that one thing?
Curly: That's what you've got to figure out.[8]

To Mitch I say the one thing, the secret of life, or the final fulfillment is the gracious truth that life is good, my life is good, the past is good, the future is good — and therefore we can say *Yes* to the fact that all is good. This is the truth of our universal spirit tradition. As long as creation goes on, this will always be the truth that sets us free. Therefore, *thankfulness* is the most authentic response of being human: being thankful for the goodness of life. "Thank-you prayers," as my granddaughter calls them, are essentially all we need to say as humans.

E. E. Cummings understood deepest gratitude in this prayerful poem, with funny punctuation:

> i thank You God for most this amazing
> day:for the leaping greenly spirits of trees
> and a blue true dream of sky;and for everything
> which is natural which is infinite which is yes
>
> (i who have died am alive again today,
> and this is the sun's birthday;this is the birth
> day of life and of love and wings:and of the gay
> great happening illimitably earth)
>
> how should tasting touching hearing seeing
> breathing any—lifted from the no
> of all nothing—human merely being
> doubt unimaginable You?
>
> (now the ears of my ears awake and
> now the eyes of my eyes are opened)[9]

From such a personal experience of universal gratitude comes the truth that will set our planet free. It is said that when Siddhartha Gautama, at the age of thirty-six, gained enlightenment under the bo (bodhi) tree, he opened his eyes to see the morning star shining in the sky and exclaimed, "How wonderful, how wonderful! . . . All beings and all things are enlightened just as they are."[10] With this nirvanic experience, he became the Buddha or "Awakened One."

If we experience "how wonderful" and say *Yes* to the way life is, then we understand that all beings and all things are good just as they are. They are in being and sustained by Being Itself. What a revolution in consciousness and ethics this awareness and life-style portend: for example, Mother Teresa's loving and serving the dying on the streets of Calcutta. She too must have experienced, as a Buddha self, that "All beings are fulfilled just as they are," and committed herself to the strange consuming power in serving the poorest of the poor.

The Happy Death

Camus' novels follow this theme of fulfillment. In *The Stranger*, Meursault says of the priest, "He wasn't even sure he was alive, because he was living like a dead man."[11] We spend too much life living as though dead. Camus' religious tradition focused him on resurrectional existence, not "living like a dead man" in this life. One of Camus' most famous figures lives the *Yes* relationship to his external situation and finds fulfillment: Sisyphus "concludes that all is well." Not as an angry or stoical or dead man, but as a happy man, Sisyphus was eternally rolling that rock up the steep incline. Camus says, "The struggle itself toward the heights is enough to fill a man's heart. One must imagine Sisyphus happy."[12]

As we live responsive to the mysterious Power at the heart of life and death, we have eternal life. The one who embraces dying everyday as a happy death has happiness in this life. The main character in his book *A Happy Death* refuses to be drugged as he dies, because he wants to experience his last moment. He wants to live his life fully by even experiencing his death. Camus says, "I do not want to believe that death is the gateway to another life," but like all experiences of life, the gateway to the full life, here and now. He sums up his understanding of real living this way:

> There are some words that I have never really understood, such as sin. . . . If there is a sin against life, it consists perhaps not so much in despairing of life as in hoping for another life and in eluding the implacable grandeur of this life.[13]

Camus, like the Buddha, has articulated the substance of fulfillment. To hope for another situation other than the one I have at this moment is most human but is not fulfilling. Fulfillment comes not from escaping the moment by hoping for another kind of moment. The unending "grandeur of this life" is found in the life I have, not in "another life." It is found in embracing the given, saying *Yes*. He has put his finger on our biggest "sin": not "despairing of life" but "eluding" or escaping life's wonder (which leads to despairing of life).

Fulfillment Is a Happy Life

As we live before Spirit at the heart of life, moving toward death, we have eternal life. *The Other World Charts* talk about fulfillment in these four ways:

> *Trek XIII*: Radical illumination — certitude at the center:
> all is clear
> *Trek XIV*: Unknowable peace — problemlessness at the
> center: nothing to hate

Trek XV: Unspeakable joy — commitment at the center:
            rapture walks with woe
Trek XVI: Endless life — eternity at the center:
            resurrectional existence

We all have experienced final fulfillment in our living. That's why fulfillment is on the chart of this life in this world and not the other life back there or out there in the future beyond this world. The promise of fulfillment is here and now for those who have been brought to see by the Spirit, and then do not run from what they see but embrace it with a committed *Yes*.

We talked about Gautama's experience. The legend goes that when he was at the gate of Nirvana he said he must not go in, but must return to guide all others to fulfillment. We remember the conversation between Pilot and Jesus. Joseph Slicker tells of Jesus' fulfillment:

> "No one takes my life from me. I lay it down." In laying it down Jesus had life. Nothing can harm him, nothing can destroy him, nothing can take his life. He is grounded in the Mystery. Or let me paraphrase Paul: "If I live, I live unto the Mystery, and if I die, I die unto the Mystery. So whether I live, or whether I die, I am the Mystery's."[14]

Since Gautama, Jesus, and Mother Teresa were persons like us, we can understand their profound experiences. We can even understand it when St. Francis kisses a leper upon the lips:

> The tears flowing from his eyes, he fell prostrate on the ground and began to kiss the soil. I remained standing above him, trembling. . . . Finally, after a long silence, he murmured with a shudder: "All these, if you kiss them on the mouth — O God, forgive me for saying this — they all . . . become Christ."[15]

And we understand it when Dostoevsky's Alyosha kisses the Earth:

> It was as though some idea had seized the sovereignty of
> his mind, and it was for all his life and for ever and ever:
> he had fallen on the earth a weak boy, but he rose up a
> resolute fighter, and he knew and felt it suddenly at the
> very moment of his ecstasy.[16]

These were experiences of fulfillment, according to the four Other
World Treks: clarity, problemlessness, centeredness, and
resurrection. Our exemplars were given to see that life is good.
They responded with a radical *Yes*. The result: my spirit is
transformed by having *said Yes to life* — not a Stoical *Yes* but an
authentic *Yes*. As Rabbi Hyman Judah Schachtel said, "Happiness
is not having what you want, but wanting what you have."

Let us remember when we have been fulfilled.

When were our *Yeses* to life transforming?
When like Buddha did we wake up and see the morning star?
When like Jesus did we make that speech to Pilot
   and experience being at one with the Mystery?
When did we care for the sick and dying,
   kiss a leper, kiss the earth and rise up fulfilled?
When did we understand not "living like a dead man"?

When did we experience . . .
The happiness of Sysiphus?
"Embracing the implacable grandeur of this life"?
Curly's "one thing"?
Or "everything which is natural which is infinite
   which is "Yes"?

When did we experiene . . .
The Kingdom of Heaven?
The kairotic moment?

That "life is good and death is good"?
And the "strange consuming happiness"
    that is there for the "ears of my ears awake"
    and "the eyes of my eyes opened"?
When did we last live unhappiness as happiness?
When did we really want the life we really had?

Fulfillment is this kind of collage that all of us have experienced as the happy life. Thanks be to Spirit!

Verse 19
Happy Death

Francis, Gandhiji, Albert, and Martin,
Joseph, Kaye, Lyn, and Liza,
Virginia, Margaret, and Mama Dotte —
they lived and died the happy death
and showed what I can do

In their lives headed toward death
brother death became
their lively, eternal guide
(hardly the last enemy)
their sanction of life
making it holier

Of course they feared
yes they were in pain
yet death did not hold them captive
he was their gracious friend
not the darkness
but the one who lit the way

They breathed the *Yes*
that to live
or to die
is to live
eternally
happy

O to live the happy death
Selah

—*september 2001*

159

Verse 20

For Elizabeth

Spirit is always home,
In life or death or beyond,
If we have the eyes to see.
The promise, *Spirit-is-with-us;*
The truth, *Spirit-is-with-us;*
The power, *Spirit-is-with-us.*

Victory is ours through Spirit.
Nothing in death or life,
In this world or any other,
In the universe high or low,
Nothing in all creation
Can separate us from Spirit.

We come from Spirit,
We live with Spirit,
We return to Spirit.
We are Thy children,
Always at home.
Blessed be Thy name forever.

We sometimes stay home,
Sometimes walk alone,
Later to return home,
Met with open arms
And great celebration,
For we are Thy children.

We come from Spirit,
We go with Spirit,
We return to Spirit —
Never far away,
Always already present.
Blessed be Thy name forever.

We live eternally,
Past, present, and future:
In Spirit eternal before,
In Spirit eternal now,
In Spirit eternal hereafter.
Blessed be Thy name forever.

We come from Spirit,
We live with Spirit,
We return to Spirit.
We give Thee back Thine own.
Give her Thy eternal rest,
Enfold her in Thy arms forever.

In Thy eternal peace
Hold her dear.
She belongs to Thee.

Hallowed be Thy name.
Thine is the kingdom,
The power, and the glory
          Forever.

—october 2001

"Labyrinth" by Ellen Howie

162

Section Three

Spirituality in the Ecozoic Era

This book is about the *profound human journey* or the *spirit journey* we are all on. Within primal communion we are awakened to, formed for, engaged in, and sustained for the *great work*, which is a life of care for creation. The *great work* is the calling that sets us free; it is the crux of spirituality. We do not "become spiritual" and then possibly take up a great work. On the contrary, we find life as we lose it in the service of a great cause that consumes us, like bringing to be the Ecozoic Era. Thomas Berry and Brian Swimme have it right:

> the future will be worked out in the tensions between those committed to . . . a future of increased exploitation of Earth as resource, all for the benefit of humans, and those committed to the Ecozoic, a new mode of human-Earth relations, one where the well-being of the entire Earth community is the primary concern (*The Universe Story*, p. 14-5).

Our human reason for being and the essential basis of the new cosmology is reverence and care for our one universal creation. The question is How do we stay motivated once we have heard the call and joined the movement of those who care for "the entire Earth community"? It's a question of deep motivation and re-motivation for sustaining the movement of movements.

Verse 21 *How Sense Emerged*

Was it the awe
        and the wonder
Amid the flare
        and the heat?

Was it the awe
        and the beauty
Amid the sound
        and the beat?

Was it the awe
        of communion
Amid the fear
        of defeat?

Was it allure
        and attraction
Amid the dark
        of the night?

Was it the tug
        of reunion
Amid the Sun's
        warming light?

How sense emerged —
        its origin?
Aye, it came by
        Spirit's might.

—*march 2002*

164

Verse 22

all things created equal?[1]

fish outswim humans
rabbits outhop humans
squirrels outclimb humans
birds outfly humans
horses outrun humans
bees outpollinate humans
viruses outmaneuver humans
rocks outmeditate humans
weather outsmarts humans
Sun outshines humans
Earth outmothers humans
life outlasts humans
Spirit outmercies humans

are humans created equal to all things?
no and yes

—august 2001

---

[1] As Thomas Berry says in a letter to a magazine editor (*What Is Enlightenment*, Fall/Winter 2001, p. 13), all elements of creation are not equal quantitatively as objects, but are equal qualitatively as subjects: "In reference to flight, the birds are on top; in reference to swimming, the fish; in reference to producing peaches, peach trees are on top. In reference to reflexive thinking, humans are on top. The important thing is that there is a single community of existence. This comprehensive community is the supreme value, not simply the human community."

Verse 23 *toward inter-everything*

from separatism to inter-being[1]

from naturalism to inter-creation
from environmentalism to inter-universe
from speciesism to inter-species

from nationalism to inter-nation
from tribalism to inter-community
from classism to inter-equality

from humanism to inter-reality
from intellectualism to inter-rationality
from scientism to inter-knowledge

from capitalism to inter-economy
from socialism to inter-wellbeing
from consumerism to inter-simplicity

from fanaticism to inter-dependence
from liberalism to inter-compassion
from conservatism to inter-preservation

from fundamentalism to inter-religious
from secularism to inter-transparency
from spiritualism to inter-spirituality[2]

what is my context
        see, change, lead
within the inter-communion[3] of all things

—*march 2001*

---

[1] Thich Nhat Hanh.   [2] Wayne Teasdale.   [3] Thomas Berry.

Reflection 11

The Cosmological Revolution: Oneness of All Creation

> Cosmology is the organization of the universe. . . . The universe is the first law of everything.[1] ~**Thomas Berry**

> Before the twentieth century we didn't even know there were other galaxies in the universe . . . thousands upon thousands of galaxies, each of which might contain ten million intelligent planets.[2]   ~**Brian Swimme**

> [W]e are seeking to reattune our cultural coding and religious symbol systems to be in touch with the genetic coding and natural systems of the universe.[3]
> ~**Mary Evelyn Tucker**

HOW WE PERCEIVE WHAT IS, how it came to be, how it is all related, and how we interpret what is, is what "cosmology" is about. Our sense of space, time, and relationships has expanded and intensified in a revolutionary way as compared with the journey of our grandparents and even our parents. There seems to be no limit to the *macrocosm* of the universe as we look outward. Similarly, there seems to be no limit to the expansion of the *microcosm* of the universe as we look down and inside. Our minds are blown both ways from the impact of how far out and how far in we can see. It's like having both a Hubble telescope and an electron microscope right in front of us. Either way, consciousness is expanded. Sometimes we glimpse what the mystics and Teilhard de Chardin meant by "Suddenly, beneath the ordinariness of our most familiar experiences, we realize . . . emerging in us is the great cosmos." We experience the truth that we are one with the most expansive and the tiniest elements of creation.

Cosmological Shifts

There have been at least three revolutionary shifts in our understanding of cosmology, of our place in the universe. Our ancestors, naively as we see now, saw themselves as the center of the universe. They were human-centered. The Middle Ages in the West still believed in the cosmology of this world and the other world of the pre-modern era wherein a supernatural power entered this world miraculously. They were otherworldly.

That two-world cosmology was done to death by the modern scientific revolution beginning in the 16th century through the industrial revolution of the 18th and 19th centuries. Galileo, Copernicus, Newton, Kepler, Bacon, and Descartes left us with a mechanistic and materialistic worldview, indicating that even though humanity is no longer the center of creation, we can manipulate creation according to our own human desires and benefit.

Beginning with Copernicus in the 16th century, who said the Earth is not the center of our solar system, we have come to understand ours as a remote planet of a solar system of a minor star off at the edge of a mammoth galaxy, which is only one of billions of galaxies in seemingly limitless space. Yet, we are still operating in a human-centered cosmology while clutching desperately for identity in the void of time and space, suggesting that we have not come to terms with reality.

The third shift has happened in my lifetime when we saw ourselves from the moon. There is absolutely no doubt that Earth is one living community, of which we humans are a most evolved and vital part, like all the other evolved and vital parts. We are becoming creation-centered. Now, in the post-modern era, we are again in a revolution in cosmology.

> Centuries ago, we thought the earth was the center of the universe. Then we discovered that the earth was going around the sun, so the sun became the center. Then we found out that the sun is moving around the galaxy, so we thought the Milky Way was the center. When we discovered that there are many galaxies, we came to the conclusion that there is no center. Finally, what we're discovering now is not that there's no center, but that every point is a center.[4]

Or all creation is the center. Brian Swimme uses the word "omnicentricity" to mean scientifically that everything in being in the universe is at the center of the ever-expanding universe.[5] Omnicentricity is a hallmark of what is called the "new cosmology" that is revolutionizing our worldview, challenging our assumptions in every way. But it will be a drawn-out revolution. For example, consider the struggle to change the human-centered language in our scriptures, hymn books, textbooks, constitutions, and secular mantras ("of, by, and for" the "people" is human-centered). Fundamental change such as this is on the way, however. I know of a few imminently qualified persons who are rewriting the U. S. Constitution to honor nonhuman rights as well as human rights.

Earthrise

Wonder and awe were the experience of the astronauts and all back on Earth as we saw the Earth from space. Since then, the Earthrise has become a spiritual symbol of our time as it connotes wholeness, oneness of creation, oneness of humanity, all with one past and one destiny.

Peter Russell talked about the single living organism of the Earth with the humorous analogy of fleas living on an elephant. They did not seem to care for the elephant until one flea leaped out far enough to see the elephant as a "living organism in its own right." The fleas' relationship to the elephant changed as the news circulated. They had a new picture of reality: the fleas came to see themselves as part of the whole system of life on the elephant. The question that got raised for the fleas was What will we do if this elephant dies? and What is our role now, having seen the big picture? Maybe they decided they'd better start caring for their elephant home.[6]

Creation as the Center

Five men have brought the cosmological revolution home to me: Albert Einstein, David Bohm, Pierre Teilhard de Chardin, Thomas Berry, and Brian Swimme. Einstein, through his relativity and quantum theories, revealed that our space-time developmental universe is one interconnected whole. Bohm, with his articulation of the implicate, explicate, and superimplicate orders of reality, has helped me to see more deeply that mystery is at the heart of the whole, "a sort of infinite reflectivity of the universe in which each part is contained in everything else."[7] Teilhard has helped restore my faith in creation in its evolution and beckons me as part of the human phenomenon to grasp my role of co-creativity. Berry and Swimme have told me the new story of the universe, from the Big Bang[8] to the present. They have told me a story that makes sense and reveals to me my vocation as a human: to walk lightly on the Earth and to live as though she is my primal community within the intercommunion of the universe.

What these scientists and historians have declared in regard to our understanding of the cosmos has revolutionary ramifications. They are guiding our emerging assumptions of the new cosmology.

Assumptions of the New Cosmology

1. The universe is our primal, sacred community.
2. Creation is in process, ever creating and recreating without end.
3. Our universe and all in it dates back c. 13-15 billion years to the "primal flaming forth" . . .
4. therefore, everything is interconnected and influences everything else.
5. Each part of creation is the center of creation . . .
6. therefore, everything is of value — full of mystery and greatness — and to be honored.
7. The universe sustains us, but even more, communes with us and nurtures us.
8. We change forms but do not go out of being.
9. Creation is good in its origin and aim, and everything in between . . .
10. therefore, we human beings are good as we are, whole, whether we feel like it or not.
11. Life is a gift; therefore, thankfulness is our second natural response.
12. Awe is our first natural response, which children know better than adults.
13. We have the freedom to decide an untold number of things.
14. We are separate yet bound.
15. We are independent within our essential, universal dependency.
16. Responsibility for all is the new morality.
17. Sacrificial care is the fundamental universe ethic.
18. Creation is an intercommunion.
19. The universe of space, time, matter, and energy is transparent to Spirit, or . . .
20. Spirit is at the heart of creation.

These benchmarks of our new cosmology seem obvious, simple, and common-sense statements. Yet, how profound they are compared with the obvious, simple, and common-sense descriptions below of operating assumptions of the *old* cosmology reigning in the West, at least.

Assumptions of the Old Cosmology

1. Creation is something that happened at the beginning . . .
2. since, the universe as a closed system has been winding down.
3. The universe is an unchanging, infinite space, even predestined.
4. Everything is separate and exclusive.
5. Creation is about 6,000 years old.
6. "Man" is the center of creation, in the "image of God."
7. Creation was created for humans . . .
8. therefore, creation is to be used as a human resource.
9. Only humans have rights.
10. Humans must defend their rights at whatever cost, even violently.
11. Humans are superior to the rest of creation.
12. Creation is sinful . . .
13. therefore, security is a major concern of the universe.
14. We are really only responsible for what "belongs" to us.
15. As individuals we are captains of our fate.
16. Power and competition are basic universal values.
17. Spirit is partial, blessing the good and cursing the bad.
18. Spirit is in another world, not here and now . . .
19. therefore, humans must work out their own salvation.
20. Matter is the essence of creation.

There is a world of difference between the *old human-centered* and *new creation-centered* lists of assumptions. Basically, in the *old,* we are over against creation or trying to manipulate creation to our advantage — aliens all, antagonists. In the *new*, we are one with creation, giving thanks for and taking care of each other in our biggest community — citizens all, protagonists. In the *old* we use and abuse creation. In the *new* we would honor and mutually enhance creation. Yet, there have been those in earlier times who have lived out of this revolutionary cosmology.

> As we know from the life of the Bushman and from the relation of the native Americans to the buffalo, the relationship between hunter and hunted is one of

reverence, of respect. . . . [They even perform rituals to the animals] whose meat becomes their life. . . . Through the next half century, the frontiersmen shot down whole herds, taking only the skins to sell and leaving the bodies to rot. This was a sacrilege. It turned the buffalo from a "thou" — to an "it."[9]   **~Joseph Campbell**

Joseph Campbell said in another interview, "Self-preservation is only the second law of life. The first law is that you and the other are one."[10] The cosmological revolution we are in revolves around this first law of oneness. Or as Thomas Berry means in the quote at the beginning, the first law is the oneness of the universe.

Our Indicative and Imperative

Paul Tillich, maybe the greatest Christian theologian of the 20th century, once said that any serious Christian is a "socialist." If he were living today, he would have moved beyond his human-centered statement to a creation-centered one and substituted for "socialist" a word like "universalist" or "creationist," but unfortunately both words have taken on a life of their own.[11]

I would change Tillich's word: any serious human is an "omnicentrist" — picking up on Brian Swimme's word above — meaning every element of creation is the center of the universe. Fundamentally, our human reason for being and the essential basis of the new cosmology is reverence and care for each element of our one universal creation. The *significance of and oneness of all creation* is our *indicative*: this paradigm is based on the way things are, the way life is: "that which is," as Augustine said. Truth has to do with our being conscious of our oneness with all creation throughout all time: that from the beginning energy became matter, which became life, which became consciousness, and the zenith of consciousness is being at one with what is.

Likewise, the oneness of all creation is our *imperative*:

the way it is, is the way it has to be. It is not just ethical to be in
relationship with the oneness of creation; if we are not, we will go
out of business as humans "doing our thing" in basic disregard of
the Earth, like myopic fleas on an elephant that dies. There is but
one Earth community of which we as humans are part. There is
not a human community that can live without the Earth community.
If we don't believe this, we are crazy, meaning not living in the
real world of the way life is: only one planetary community in one
universe. Of course there are subcommunities, but all are
interdependent and all are dependent upon the Earth community,
which is dependent upon the universe community.

I like the way Connie Barlow and Michael Dowd say it:

> [K]nowledge of the cosmos is, in a very real sense, self
> knowledge. We are not separate beings *in* the Universe,
> who live *on* Earth. We are a mode of being *of* the Uni-
> verse, an expression *of* Earth. We didn't come into this
> world, we grew out from it.[12]

"Oneness of all creation" is the cosmological truth that is
the first law of our one community Earth. That which is not in
sync with cosmology's indicative/imperative truth will reap the
whirlwind, for the new common sense of this revolution says there
is no protection for those who violate the universal truth of unity
and wholeness.

On a note of cosmological hope, Thomas Berry writes:

> Evidence for this hopefulness [peace of Earth] is found
> in the sequence of *crisis moments* through which the
> universe and, especially, the planet Earth have passed
> from the beginning until now. At each state of its devel-
> opment, when it seems that an impasse has been reached,
> most improbable solutions have emerged that enabled the
> Earth to continue its development. . . . This story of the
> past provides our most secure basis of hope that the

> Earth will so guide us through the peril of the present
> that we may provide a fitting context for the next phase
> of the emergent mystery of earthly existence.[13]

No one doubts that we live in such a moment of crisis. What can save us is a deepened communion with the Earth, and everything on it, spinning within our primordial and destinal universe. Neither self, family, nations, religions, nor even human civilization is a big enough context to live before or on behalf of.

> We might think of the threefold evolutionary process: the
> galactic evolutionary processes of the universe, the geo-
> biological evolutionary processes of Earth, and the cul-
> tural evolutionary processes of the human that need to be
> understood in their sacred dimension. These are the three
> components of the single evolutionary narrative. . . .[14]

These three evolutionary processes making up the single evolutionary narrative are the context propelling the cosmological revolution we are now in. Any reduction of this *oneness-of-all-creation* context spells trouble for all species of Earth, including the human.

What a process. What a destiny. Truly awesome.

Verse 24 *By Cosmic Design?*

Watching young people
gape as they hear Thomas say
the U.S. Constitution is destructive
declaring only human rights
or hearing him ask
now that western civilization
has passed through its religious
and humanist phases
what next

On its way forward through the past
the next cosmological age
accentuates awesome seasons
that birth rituals
and daily sunrises and sunsets
that spiritize existence
sanctifying early mornings
with meditation
and evenings with
family reverie
      parents cuddled up
      reading to their children
      answering big questions
      rubbing backs and humming
      as their little ones pass into
      the dark, sacred night of dreams

Are we spiritual
by cosmic design
and for cosmic reasons?

—*april 2001 at Timberlake Farm*

176

Verse 25

Go Fly

with Stephen Hawking
we will mount our wheelchairs
decked out with mega voice
with his smile and wit
flying his cosmology
far out, deep, and wide

we will get perspective
on where we came from
and where we go
relearning our name
and place

'Who am I' is a massive think
with the deepest feel
of 'what be I'
and mighty resolve
of 'what do I'

I am 'who I am' in the universe
so let me, myself, and I
go fly
and come back to Earth
I-mazed

—*august 2001*

Verse 26

Nature Teaches Us

We learn . . .
      awe through lightning
      beauty through flowers
      majesty through mountains
      fear through thunder
      leadership from geese
      teamwork from ants
      parenting from elephants
      visioning from eagles
      maneuvering from viruses
      communication from dolphins
We learn . . .
      love through offsprings
      forgiveness from dogs
      community from bees
      ingenuity from beavers
      tenacity from squirrels
      sacrifice from crops
      wonder through spiderwebs
      contentment from cows
      curiosity from cats
      play from monkeys
We learn . . .
      warmth from Sun
      hard work from mules
      direction from waterways
      force from hurricanes
      mystery through night skies

    marvel through butterflies
    power through wind
    cleansing through rain
    transformation through caterpillars
    peace through snow
We learn . . .
    extinction from dinosaurs
    risk through planting
    calm from trees
    praise from birds
    endurance from camels
    terror through fires
    endlessness through waves
    relaxation from bears
    finitude through earthquakes
    defense through predators
We learn . . .
    dying from Fall
    death from Winter
    resurrection from Spring
    nourishment from Summer
    interdependence through eating
    union through breeding
    connectedness through vistas
    dependence through breathing
    reflection through night
    anticipation through dawn

We learn the reverence of intercommunion
Seeing Spirit through nature's transparent veil.

—*march 2002*

Reflection 12

The Great Work Movement:
Creating the Ecozoic Era

> [W]e must persist in the quest for united action to counter both global warming and a weaponized world. . . . To survive in the world . . . we must learn to think in a new way. As never before, the future of each depends on the good of all.[1] **~100 Noble Laureates**, December 7, 2001

The phrase "the great work," the name of the latest book by Thomas Berry, has captivated many because it has pronounced the consensus that we all knew but did not know until someone like Thomas said it. That's the role of the poet or the sage. Thomas has been talking like this for decades, relentlessly saying what has needed to be said until we believe. We have been waiting all our lives for someone to call us to *the great work*.

Neither economic, political, or cultural movements will deal with that which divides us as a planet. We do not seem to be sustained as before by our cultural stories, our religious beliefs, or our national constitutions. What is needed is not more and better from the old social vehicle and the old religious mode, but a new spirit mode for the planet that universally sustains and unites. Depth quality of life will not come from bigger GNPs, more religious institutions, finer universities, more efficient governments, and the like. None of them will save us or finally unite us six billion humans and all other beings on planet Earth.

We all know that quality of life is not about more or less

of this or that, but about a new spirituality among us

> that *believes* Spirit is always already present
> that *sees* creation is good
>   and evolution is always possible
> that *hears* the planetary call
> and *knows* down deep
>   that the quest is worth our lives
>   that we have all we need to care for all
>   that the one spirit movement is emerging
> in which every individual longs
> to be part of the great work
> of building the Earth.

What it will take for us humans to care authentically for this planet in this universe is *the* spiritual issue of our time.

And we sense that engaging in such a great work will fulfill us personally. I am not only advocating a personal spiritual journey in this book but also a planetary spiritual movement, one that would engage us all in care of creation.

Our Great Work

To update John Donne's poem, "No human is an island, entire of itself; every human is a piece of the planet, a part of the universe. If terrorism further maims our planetary community, if soil be washed away because of no trees, we all are the less. Any species' death diminishes me; and therefore never send to know for whom the bell tolls; it tolls for thee" — it tolls for all.

We are not only our brother's keeper, we are our river's keeper. How do we begin to communicate to our young people, in a way that they will not forget, that their great work is to show reverence for creation, including human reconciliation. The other species seem to operate out of such reverence, at least mutual respect. I can imagine Albert Schweitzer saying as a young man, "If reverence for life seems irrelevant, it is because it has been poorly presented. I will change that." Our great work is to care for the Earth our whole lives just as she cares for us. We are to sacrifice for her as she does for us.

We remember those walks in the woods, those times at the beach when we contemplate the rolling waves as sublime gifts of the universe to us. Can we imagine what it is like to live in the highest village in the Himalayas and to be awed by that view each day? I have looked at and off the Blue Ridge Mountains of Virginia and North Carolina — one of our oldest ranges — throughout my life and have been deeply awed. Such beauty calls us back to intimate care for all creation, the fundament of our great work.

The great work is no longer a noble ideal. As Sun Tzu reminds us in *The Art of War*, we are now on "death ground," surrounded by enemies on every side who seemingly will fight to the death. The 100 Nobel Laureates named two of the enemies "global warming" and the "weaponized world," rightly pointing to double-pronged natural and human disaster. This is a new day. As the Earth and its atmosphere go, so goes humanity. As Berry says, if our life raft the Earth goes, why worry about all other concerns? For we are one body, one flesh, one planetary community in one universe. Our unity is our gift and our demand. "One for all and all for one," or "We all go down together": old sayings, still true.

We have to create new strategies and tactics to be about the business of caring powerfully and responsibly for the intercommunion we are. We must stand guard against the ravages of economic interests who have forgotten that the bell tolls for them, also, especially if they abuse the rights of the Earth. Let us be clear that the rights of the Earth take precedence over any nation's, corporation's, or individual's rights. And we must take responsibility for any who shirk their responsibility. No longer can we humans stand by and watch anyone rape our Earth community.

The great work of caring for creation is our vocation, our calling, the major theme of our lives, both out of great love and great necessity. We find our fulfillment in the Earth's fulfillment. Mutual fulfillment is the only way.

Context for a New Spirit Mode

Berry says that nothing makes sense unless it enhances the "intercommunion with the total range of reality,"[2] or "nothing is without everything else." He gives the context in his "Twelve Principles For Understanding the Universe and the Role of the Human in the Universe Process"[3] to help us frame the new spirit mode coming into being:

> 1. The universe [is] . . . the primary revelation of that ultimate mystery whence all things emerge into being.
> 2. [E]ach being of the planet is profoundly implicated in the existence and functioning of every other being of the planet.
> 3. [T]he universe is a psychic[4] as well as a physical reality.
> 5. The universe . . . is consistently creative.
> 6. The human is that being in whom the universe activates, reflects upon, and celebrates itself in conscious self-awareness.
> 12. The main human task of the immediate future is to assist in activating the inter-communion of all the living and non-living components of the earth community.

Operating out of these principles, the old religious mode and old social vehicle would be transformed.[5] The "spiritual-physical intercommunion of the parts with each other, with the whole, and with that numinous presence which has ever been manifested throughout this entire cosmic-earth-human process"[6] is the "the ontological covenant of the universe."[7] To say the least, our new spirit mode would find us bowing to all others in authentic mutual appreciation.

The Spirit Movement

> The Great Work before us . . . is not a role that we have chosen. It is a role given to us, beyond any consultation with ourselves. . . . We were chosen by some power beyond ourselves for this historical task. . . . The nobility of our lives . . . depends upon the manner in which we come to understand and fulfill our assigned role.[8] **~Thomas Berry**

What are some new strategies for the great work movement? "[C]ommunity-supported agriculture, solar-hydrogen energy system, redesign of our cities, elimination of the automobile in its present form, restoration of local village economies, education for a post-petroleum way of life, and a jurisprudence that recognizes the rights of natural modes of being."[9] "[A]ny recovery of the natural world in its full splendor will require not only a new economic system but a conversion experience deep in the psychic structure of the human."[10] Thomas points to *Our Way Into the Future*, the subtitle of *The Great Work,* and names the movement:

> History is governed by those overarching movements that give shape and meaning to life by relating the human venture to the larger destinies of the universe. Creating such a movement might be called the Great Work of a people.[11]

This *great work movement, intercommunion movement, spirit movement,* is being created by those who are about caring for all of creation. We know there are hundreds of movements abroad that are comprehensive. One could even call the United

Nations a movement and applaud its recent fifteen-year plan for the Earth community. But none of these is *the* movement.

> Robert Nisbet, social analyst, wrote in 1982, it is entirely possible that when the history of the twentieth century is finally written, the single most important social movement of the period will be judged to be environmentalism. . . . [T]he environmentalist cause has become today almost a mass movement, its present objective little less than the transformation of government, economy, and society in the interest of what can only be properly called the liberation of nature from human exploitation. Environmentalism is now well on its way to becoming the third great wave of the redemptive struggle in Western history, the first being Christianity, the second modern socialism. In its way, the dream of a perfect physical environment has all the revolutionary potential that lay both in the Christian vision of mankind redeemed by Christ and in the socialist, chiefly Marxian, prophecy of mankind free from social injustice.[12]
> **~Kathleen Marquardt**

The great work movement will make all the difference, bound together in some loose but self-conscious network of care for the future life of the Earth, its constituents, and its atmosphere.

What is the vision of such a movement? To bring into being what we now call, using Berry's phrase, the Ecozoic Era, the "new mode of human-Earth relations, one where the well-being of the entire Earth community is the primary concern."[13] This *great work* is our new human destiny, our common vocation. This is the movement of Spirit in our time.[14]

Verse 27

Spirit Movement

Who can stop a movement on which every being's life depends?
Who can stop a movement that is history long, universe wide,
      and spirit deep?
Who can stop a movement with a membership of all peoples,
      all cultures, and all religions?
Who can stop a movement that's out to protect every being's home,
      every being's rights, and every being's spirit?
Who can stop a movement that's the big tent for all caring
      movements of our planetary community?

Beware of trying to stop this movement.
Be enhanced by advancing it.
It's a movement whose time has come.
It's a movement worth body and soul,
      for it's the spirit movement of intercommunion.

The *Spirit*, the *story*, the *urgency*, the *call* — all these —
      and *we* are creating this movement.
May we be so motivated ever and again
      in this the movement of Spirit in our time.
To be in this movement, this *great work*, is to be fulfilled,
      for it's about the fulfillment of creation.[15]

Verse 28 *Uni-verse*

one beat
one heart
one life

her pulse rate beeps and flashes
as she lies post-surgery
aping body Universe

one beat
one heart
one life

beating out her rhythm
in the citadel of time
from the beginning till now

one beat
one heart
one life

humans we are not except
as universal beings
in the planetary rite

one beat
one heart
one life

gi-ven
for all
en masse

—*february 4, 2002, TCC Hospital, Galax, Virginia*

Verse 29

"Just Do It" Can't Do It Alone

Out of nothing comes something, every time.
That's the way it is, *just watch it.*
> Out of cosmic crisis came the air we breathe;
> Out of slavery comes freedom;
> Out of death comes life.
That's the way it is, *just trust it.*

Out of terrorism will come global unity.
That's the way it is, *just weld it.*
> Out of poverty will come equity;
> Out of AIDS will come global health;
> Out of biocide will come planetary care.
That's the way it is, *just spawn it.*

Out of powerlessness comes power, every time.
That's the way it is, *just free it.*
> Spirit brings something out of nothing,
> Not by a zap but sacrifice —
> Some being's offering that changes things.
That's the way it is, *just give it.*

Just do it
can't do it
alone.

—june 2001

189

Verse 30 *Journeyed*

As a proud human being
I tell myself I am
in charge of my journey.
Like pilgrims of yore
I do spiritual practices
and journey spiritual paths
that lead on the way
to the mountain top
and to perfection.

But when I look back on my life
I see I have been journeyed
by that which journeys all.
In each encounter
I experience beatitudes
of the awesome way:
reflection
interpretation
and thanksgiving.

As a theologian[1] said
in a better moment:
"If it took *all that*
to bring me to *this moment*,
I wouldn't change a thing."

—august 2001

---

[1] Marilyn Monroe to reporters during "this moment" of happiness when marrying Arthur Miller. Maybe the "all that" was her being born an illegitimate child, her earliest memory of her mother's trying to smother her with a pillow, and her mother's being institutionalized; Marilyn's living in foster homes, raped at age eleven and assaulted many times as an early teen, a couple of divorces, drug dependence most of her adult life, an alleged affair with the President, and being a sex idol. That's all.

190

Reflection 13

The Profound Human Journey

[A]uthentic spirituality is . . . revolutionary.[1] ~**Ken Wilber**

THE PROFOUND HUMAN JOURNEY, or the spirit journey, is the life we are created for, the life of being thankful for and continuing creation. Most of us humans most of the time do not live the human journey profoundly. Yet occasionally we all do.

The *profound human journey dynamics*[2] are 1) communion, 2) awakenment, 3) formation, 4) engagement, and 5) sustenance. They are not necessarily sequential as numbered but dynamically interactive.

We begin our journey as Spirit communes with us, awakens us, forms us, engages us, and sustains us in our great journey of care. Spirit is the origin, center, and omega point for the good creation. Spirit started the journey, has been recreating it all the way, and is now changing our hearts as we enter the next phase of care for the whole Earth.

Dynamic One — Community: The Great Communion

We are creatures made for the *great communion*. We experienced it after September 11 as we came together like seldom in a lifetime, as we reached out to care for each other in heroic and small ways across the globe. We experienced that deep urge within to be in community, to be connected, to be family, to be at one with the other.

191

Thomas Berry writes, "In and through this [universe] community we enter into communion with that numinous mystery whence all things depend for their existence and their activity."[3] Permeating time, space, matter, and energy is the numinous mystery of communion, without which the four are but so much stuff. With the presence of Spirit, they are enlivened: once an *it*, now a *thou*. Spirit makes all the difference.

The *great communion* keeps humans honoring creation by saying, "I give thanks for your being." In India, with hands pressed together, people bow to greet each other with "Namaste," meaning, "I bow to the presence of Spirit revealed through you." We are reminded by this simple greeting that every piece of creation is transparent to Spirit and is therefore sacred. This is the essential expression of what I mean by the *great communion*: we see and come to experience the reality of Spirit, whether it be through a child's joy, a butterfly's circuitous flight, or in the aftermath of global acts of terrorism.

If *all* is transparent to Spirit, then we have the foundation for the community of all beings, who are kin to us because we all are creatures revealing Spirit, our common denominator. With the gift of this awareness, we begin to understand how the *great communion* blesses creation.

And when we are asked what is our purpose for being, we might recite out of an updated catechism, "to love and glorify Spirit forever, and all that it journeys, unites, and sustains." The *great communion* is with the Spirit that meets us in creation.

I have experienced the dynamic of *profound community* throughout my life. A few examples are
- being raised in a loving family and living now with a loving family
- being raised in a small town
- being sustained by a powerful covenant in marriage

- living in Muslim and Hindu villages and American ghettos
- living in a pluriform, secular-religious family Order
- flying down the Shenandoah Valley and experiencing an overpowering sense of oneness with creation as my home

Reflect upon your own **communion** *examples. . . .*

Dynamic Two — Awakenment: The Great Event

We all experience the *great event*.

The great event has happened to me innumerable times, in big and small ways. Once it happened when I was about fifteen in the mountains of Virginia, trying to figure out how I was going to live with only one eye after the accident. I was distraught and feeling especially sorry for myself as I lay there in the hospital room in Roanoke, Virginia, with big bandages over both eyes. A woman came up next to my bed and gently took my hand. She asked if she might pray for me. I consented. After the prayer I felt brand new, like I was all right, that I would be just fine no matter what happened. Changed in a moment. Yes. Did I see again out of that eye? No. Did I ever despair again over my condition? Of course. But at that moment I will never forget that I knew a strange peace. This is only one of hundreds of such gracious moments I can recount, and not even the most awesome.

New life with new consciousness breaks in. We are the same but with a changed heart, as Judaism describes it. And if we accept the fact of our acceptance and say *Yes*, sometimes we experience being put back together again.

This is creation's *great event* that belongs to no one and happens to everyone. To call it religious is quite understandable but not necessary. The *great event* reminds us that life is on our side, always given and always to be received, thankfully.

The *great event* reveals what really is. What was not apparent suddenly shows through. Transparently, we are given to see clearly the truth that all creation is good, that life is good, and that we are good — not because of anything we have done or not done — but simply because we are part of the good and grace-filled creation. This transforming truth is made known to us in the *great event*.

   We must be awakened to the glory of the profound human journey we are on; we do not achieve it. *Awakenment* is a gift.

I have experienced the dynamic of *profound awakenment* throughout my life. A few examples are

- as a youth during a retreat near Asheville, North Carolina
- waking up when JFK was assassinated
- experiencing awesome freedom at a clergy colloquy taught by the Ecumenical Institute in Richmond, Virginia
- barely escaping death in a auto accident south of Milwaukee on I-94
- seeing the movie *Gandhi* after living in India
- reading Thomas Berry's *Befriending the Earth* and hearing the call to the great work

Reflect upon your own **awakenment** *examples. . . .*

Dynamic Three — Formation

We are spiritually prepared through *formation* — between *awakenment* and *engagement* — when we are made ready to do the great work. After being awakened we are often called to prepare ourselves as we covenant with That which journeys us. Between the vocational call and the great work is the dynamic of *formation*, or getting "formed," getting prepared.

   How do we prepare a person to lead a people to build the Earth? How do we get a Moses trained to lead a people through the wilderness for forty years? How do we get a Gandhi trained to free India? How do we get a Teresa trained to care for those dying in the streets of the cities? How do we get a Mandela trained to reconcile a nation? Their interiors were formed through soulful reflections on the experiences and mysteries of life.

This world knows exemplary formation models: journeying girls and boys to become leaders of the church and religious orders, journeying boys to be the Dalai Lama, journeying boys to become samurai warriors, journeying boys to become kings and girls to become queens.

Those helping to train persons for the great work must be about the great work themselves, and must create and use transformative methods. Ignatius of Loyola, founder of the Society of Jesus (Jesuits), knew that the Xaviers who followed him could not stand in their great work on the other side of the world for a lifetime without incredible interior formation. Therefore, he prepared them foundationally, as "pillars of iron" (Jeremiah 1:18-19), knowing that one leads the ten who train the hundred who catalyze the thousands. And Ignatius sent them out with the now-famous Ignatian model for their regular retreats, which took them to the center of being and back annually. It seems to have worked. What does a similarly profound model of formation look like today?

The *awakened* are called to be about the great work of our time. How do we call forth and train profound leaders? How do we insure they will not crash and burn early on in their noble endeavors? What are the formation structures and methods persons need to stand as pillars of iron for a lifetime of service?

I have experienced the dynamic of *profound formation* throughout my life. A few examples are

- spending much time as a youth at my church's youth center
- reading about my saints: *i.e.*, Bonhoeffer, Gandhi, Woolman
- being journeyed by mentors Joseph and Lyn Mathews and colleagues of the Order: Ecumenical
- learning how to build and sustain community in that same Order
- participating in the eight-week Academy program of the Institutes that was a transformative formation structure
- writing my memoir about my spirit journey

*Reflect upon your own **formation** examples. . . .*

Dynamic Four — Engagement: The Great Work

As we said in Reflection 12 about the "Great Work Movement," we are commandeered for *engagement*, even like unto a true soldier's call to duty to defend his people and all he holds dear in his engagement unto death on their behalf. This time our commission is bigger: through the *engagement* in *the great work* we are sent to free humanity for creation-centered living.

We are being grasped by a new vision of reality and are beginning to create a disciplined style as individuals and as a human community to care for that which is our gift and our sacred responsibility. In our hearts we are stewards, guardians, caretakers in covenant with creation.

Mutual care by creation for creation is the only way. If the Earth comes off, so do we. If it doesn't, neither do we. If human reconciliation comes off, so do we. If it doesn't, neither do we. Our *great work* seems so clear. Its first law is that progress is measured by unity. If races, cultures, and religions are honoring each other, if economic and political structures are honoring all species' basic rights, and if we in our communities and homes are showing direct compassion and love for each other, then the great work is happening. Progress is measured by unity.

I have experienced the dynamic of *profound engagement* throughout my life. A few examples are
- selling our house, car, books, and furnishings to join the Order: Ecumenical for nearly two decades of global service
- living with the poor and marginalized to help them in their comprehensive development
- living and working with numerous nationalities, races, cultures, and religions, sharing spirit journey methods
- being deeply engaged in the care of my local community, especially downtown Galax
- being engaged in the *great work* movement with the likes of

Thomas Berry and the Center for Ecozoic Studies through seminars, bioregional networking, writing, and a new compassion for our biggest community

Reflect upon your own **engagement** *examples. . . .*

Dynamic Five — Sustenance

In the midst of *community* one is *awakened* to, *formed* for, and *engaged* in *the great work*. How does s/he stick to it day after day, being out there where one intends to be? What *sustains* one for the dark night and the long march?

There will come holy humiliation, *à la* St. John of the Cross in *The Dark Night of the Soul and the Flaming Fire of Love,*[4] which is, he testifies, the foundation for the profound human journey. During such humiliation, when "progress" doesn't work, when we are wiped out by our own human intentions, the deepest questions arise: What is the meaning of it all? Can I/we go on? St. John answers that through the deep pain of humiliation, weakness, abandonment, and wretchedness comes authentic strength for the journey.

Does any of this make sense today? To modernize St. John's message:

Society and I were cruising along
When something happened
An alien image darkened all, wiped out what was
We were blinded by the glare of the future
    which will never be the same as the past
Yet, in it all a strange motivation — in spite of us —
    beckons us toward a radical destiny of care

This radical destiny is calling forth, forming, engaging, and sustaining new spirit leaders for the great work. It is not for the faint of heart, this transforming journey. Don't forget how many times Gandhi fasted and was imprisoned to change his India; don't forget the twenty-seven years that Mandela was imprisoned.

The refiner's fire, if it doesn't kill us, might just purify and forge us to change history. St. John suggests the *long march* will inevitably land us in vocational crisis: Is all I've been doing for nothing? We will experience rootlessness, ineffectivity, loneliness, and unfulfillment. Still, we are called and sent to care.

But strangest of all, when we are ready to quit, we sometimes begin to see the way, in the hell we are experiencing. The fire transforms. Darkness is lit. We sometimes hear, "You are the one with whom I am well pleased." And, sometimes, we are at one with That which put us in Its seemingly hopeless situation to begin with.

Wilber says, "radical transformation . . . in short, [is] not a conventional bolstering of consciousness but a radical transmutation and transformation at the deepest seat of consciousness itself."[5] "Profound" means transformation as individuals, caring groups, communities, and movements.

The *dark night* and the *long march* are the shakedown part of the profound human journey. In spite of all, we experience that we are sustained, received, united, even loved by Being Itself; and that we are free to decide to be who we are — as our greatest illusions are being trodden to nought — and free to decide to care for creation over and over again.

I have experienced the dynamic of *profound sustenance* throughout my life. A few examples are
- growing up in a faith community
- being sustained through periods of deep despair
- *meditation*: dialogue, reading, journaling, breathing, writing
- *contemplation*: communion with creation directly and through art
- *prayer*: reflection, thanksgiving, intercession, dedication
- compassionate and tough love from family, friends, and mission-colleagues

- my present mission of writing and movement involvement
Reflect upon your own **sustenance** *examples. . . .*

In Sum

We have lived long enough, have lived through enough, to understand Wilber's quote at the beginning of this Reflection: "[A]uthentic spirituality is . . . revolutionary," or the authentic spirit journey is transformative — life changing and life consuming.

> [A]ny realization of depth carries a terrible burden: Those who are allowed to see are simultaneously saddled with the obligation to *communicate* that vision in no uncertain terms: that is the bargain. . . . It is your duty to speak your truth with whatever passion and courage you can find in your heart.[6]   **~Ken Wilber**

This is the mandate for all on the profound human journey on behalf of creation.

Through profound *communion, awakenment, formation, engagement,* and *sustenance* we journey on into the deeper meaning of existence. There is no retirement. There is no end to the profound human journey. We all are on it, some more self-consciously than others. It is the way that blesses all, for It is Spirit's way. As we said in the beginning,

> THE PROFOUND HUMAN JOURNEY, or the spirit journey, is the life we are created for, the life of being thankful for and continuing creation.

Verse 31

Spirit Does Not Promise . . .[1]

long life
good health
financial security
a marriage that works
loving children
a nice house
a solid job
sweet dreams
no pain
a good education
kind in-laws
responsible government
safe cities
no taxes
good neighbors
and world peace

. . . but Spirit does promise

abundant life
grace sufficient for every need
forgiveness when we deserve none
peace that passes understanding
balm for the deepest grief
a calling whether we want it or not
courage in spite of fear
more freedom than we want

refuge amid raging storms
rest for the weary
hope against hope
light in the darkest night
joy unspeakable
welcome home with open arms
resurrection in this life
love that will not let us go
Its eternal presence

. . . and believe it or not, Spirit does promise

ways to end poverty, stop wars, and save the Earth

---

[1]Adapted from *Motivation for the Great Work*, pp. 75-6.

Verse 32 *Gifts of the Spirit*

Tell me why there is something and not nothing
Tell me why some-thing comes from no-thing

Tell me why some things are better than others
Such as

Being is better than not being
Mystery is better than knowledge
Consciousness is better than stupor
Grace is better than achievement
Communion is better than separation
Faith is better than beliefs
Freedom is better than bondage
Mercy is better than law
Love is better than hate
Care is better than care less
Vocation is better than work
Community is better than self-worship
Peace is better than war
Fulfillment is better than rewards
Happiness is better than existing

Tell me why these are quality-of-life things
                heart desires
Not things to consume, store, and throw away

But really tell me why the real things in life are free
            and the rest we have to buy

—*4/8/2001 nac's 3rd birthday*

Reflection 14

Practical Spirituality: Assuming Spirit Is Always Already Present

¶There is ... nothing but Spirit in all directions. ... [T]here is no place where Spirit is not. .... [T]here is no space lacking, and there is no space more full. There is only Spirit. ¶It will not do to say that Spirit is present but I don't realize it. That would require the Great Search. .... [S]eeking misses the present.

¶You and I are already convinced that there are things that we need to do in order to realize Spirit. We feel that there are places that Spirit is not (namely, in me), and we are going to correct this state of affairs. ...

¶The Great Search is the search for an ultimate experience, a fabulous vision, a paradise of pleasure, unendingly good time, a powerful insight — a search for God, a search for Goddess, a search for Spirit — but Spirit is not an object. ¶Our awareness is clouded with some form of avoidance. ... [W]e want to run away from it, or run after it, or we want to change it, alter it, hate it, love it, loathe it, or in some way agitate to get ourselves into, or out of, it. ...

¶Somehow, no matter what your state, you are immersed fully in everything you need for perfect enlightenment. ... One hundred percent of Spirit is in your perception right now. ...

¶Spirit is the only thing that has never been absent. [1]

~Ken Wilber

IS SPIRITUALITY PRACTICAL AND PRACTICABLE? No
and yes. *No*, spirituality is not something that comes with
practice, as Wilber so forcefully says. In fact, the more we search,
the more we close ourselves to Spirit's reality, or the less in
communion with Spirit we are, negating the fact that It is always
absolutely present.

But there is a paradox here. I must also say, *Yes*, Spirit's
presence becomes more conscious to us through practice. I am
choosing my words very carefully here, for there has been much
confusion in the past about spiritual practices, and seemingly even
more today as this spirit revolution mounts. Said more directly,
we operate out of deep-seated illusion in our attempt to "become
spiritual." I hear Wilber saying we just *are* spiritual but have a
hard time accepting it, since we have been programmed to seek
something or do something to become spiritual.

One thing must be said at this point that is all-important:
since Spirit *is* ever-present and since we *are* spiritual (period),
then practical spirituality takes place in all we do, know, and be,
in the very midst of our everyday, real lives. Spirituality is not for
the few who live set-apart lives who pray all day, as it were. Any
of us can do that, as Brother Lawrence pointed out as he worked
in the monastery kitchen, *practicing the presence* — one of the
best descriptions of the self-conscious spirit journey. Of course a
monk is spiritual, also, but not any more spiritual than the rest of
us. He/she may be more conscious of Spirit's presence, but he
can't be any more spiritual, because we are all equally spiritual,
living the same spirit journey called existence. All this is true if
the ever-present Spirit is always at hand and therefore equally
close to every being.

Practical spirituality happens where we are, at work, with
the family, in church, at the movies, at the beach, in a meeting, at
school, in the shower, in bed; practical spirituality *happens in what
we're doing*, whether seeing, hearing, touching, tasting, smelling,

dialoguing, dreaming, writing, calculating, walking, swimming, having sex; practical spirituality *happens in what we're reflecting on*, praying, cogitating, mulling, and brooding over, weighing up, deciding, contemplating, meditating; practical spirituality *happens in what we're being*, confused, joyful, sorrowful, despairing, provoked, called, resistant, surrendering.

We are spiritual in and throughout our everyday, real lives. That's not to say we are not blind to, unaware of, or willfully closed to Spirit more times than not, but we *are* spiritual nonetheless, whether we are saying *Yes* or *No* or *Don't know*. We *are* spiritual because of the always already present Spirit in our lives that we will never get away from — our dance partner till the day we die. Because of that fact, life is sacramental, a spirit journey from dust to dust.

One more thing before we consider practical spiritual practices: we have said throughout this book that the spirit journey is not for one's personal sake so much as for the sake of creation. We are not so much about a personal spiritual goal of some kind as about being creation's servant. Here is where spiritual sustenance is demanded, as we talked about the Reflection 13 ("Profound Human Journey"), especially in the dark night and long march. In the great work, we will burn to a cinder or try to leave the journey (try to commit "spiritocide"[2]) for any number of reasons, and some we will think are justifiable. But since we *can't* leave the spirit journey, we *can* say *No,* become victim to the journey, and be dragged all the way against our will — cursing and denying fulfillment. The promise throughout the annals of spirituality is that we are fulfilled when we *willingly* are on Spirit's journey, present with open eyes and a big *Yes*, because being guided by and following Spirit is what we were created to know, do, and be.

Spirit Practice Parameters

With this context, some parameters for practical spiritual

sustenance are in order.

I have written of the four stages of development for us humans: as I see it, the spiral of the human journey stages are 1) *self-focused*, 2) *ethno-focused* (family, tribe, religion, civilization biases: for example, "Western"), 3) *human-focused* (a focus on humans and humanity in general — and September 11 has pushed us all more deeply toward this focus), and 4) *creation-focused* (humans caring for the planetary community, at least).

Spirit guides us through all four stages of the human journey. There is not a spirit-focused fifth stage. Spirit is the warp and woof of all the stages. Spirit is at the heart of the dynamics of creation. This is akin to what I mean by Teilhard's word "cosmogenesis": the eternal process of co-creation by every bit of creation. Spirit sustains, awakens, forms, engages, and unites selves, tribes, humanity, and creation without end, and in so doing Spirit journeys and uses us all as Its instruments.

The goal of the human journey, therefore, is not for us to sit and wait for Spirit but to be guided by It. We are to develop into Spirit-sensitives, always attentive and ready in every situation, whether in personal meditation or mediating peace. The Spirit-sensitive person in all four stages seeks to help others to see that the stages of self-, ethno-, homo-, and cosmo-focus are all blessed stages; the Spirit-aware person is free and called to live in response to the ever-present Spirit that encounters us *throughout* the human journey; and the Spirit-conscious person is always being sent to live passionately on behalf of all that is. In other words, the spiritual life is not a developmental destination but a journey-long, gracious encounter. Spirit elicits our *Yes* as It calls and sends us into the service of all. Needless to say, our spirit journey can be profound and glorious at every stage because of Spirit's presence.

Spirituality is practical more than it is religious, that is, if it is an everyday reality concerned with living the fulfilled life in whatever stage of the journey one is in: whether that of a wise spiritual leader like the Dalai Lama, who is encouraging the global religious to care for creation, or whether that of young children who have the eyes of wonder and the hearts of compassion.

Whatever stage we're in, deep practical questions face us: How do we take care of ourselves on the spirit journey? How do we keep reminded that we *are* spiritual and not seeking to be spiritual? How do we stay awake to the ever-present Spirit? How do we live the life-style of intercommunion with creation and Spirit? How do we prepare ourselves to be Spirit's effective instruments?

Chart of Creation-Centered Exercises

Moving toward creation-centered spiritual exercises is the indicative direction for our spirit journeys. Below is a simple yet comprehensive framework for considering our practical spirit journey: first, the four stages; second, another simple yet comprehensive framework — knowing, doing, and being. When we mesh the two frameworks, we come up with a four-by-three chart, which would hold a minimum of twelve spiritual practices. Although I include twelve examples, the comprehensive titles for our spiritual practices[3] are the thing to hold in mind. Then, anyone, with some deliberation, can fill in practices for himself or for a group or movement. We are moving toward creation-centeredness, as Spirit would have it.

MOVING TOWARD CREATION-CENTERED SPIRITUAL EXERCISES

	Knowing	Doing	Being
Self	Meditation (1. autobio writing)	Prayer (2. care beads)	Contemplation (3. personal montage)
Tribe	Community (4. storytelling)	Vocation (5. life-lining)	Sacraments (6. spirit conversation)
Humanity	Inter-community (7. 200+ nations)	Social Vehicle (8. three things)	Communion of Saints (9. inner council)
Creation	Inter-species (10. universe walk)	Great Work (11. eco-circle)	Intercommunion (12. creation vigil)

Descriptions of Twelve Creation-centered Exercises

Self-focused

1. (K) *Autobiographical Writing*: writing about one's life, from a journal to a memoir
2. (D) *Care Beads*: ritualistically touching beads on a string (homemade, even), each representing one's cares, from one's mother or grandchildren to a conflict like the Middle East to dying species on the planet
3. (B) *Personal Montage*: constructing a montage of one's journey through pictures

Tribe-focused

4. (K) *Storytelling*: the Swamp Gravy[4] method is a good example, wherein one shares a little life story; the listener then tells it to the group that did not hear it
5. (D) *Life-Lining*: creating a personal timeline that goes far enough into the future to call forth one's vocational intent
6. (B) *Spirit Conversation*: in this case, a conversation in a group about major turning points in one's journey, using as a guide life's sacraments: for example, births, covenants, deaths

Human-focused

7. (K) *200+ Nations*: after this Reflection is a list of the nations of the globe, which one can repeat and even try to memorize, to bring to consciousness
8. (D) *If I Were the Leader of the Earth, Three Things I Would Command*: this exercise allows us to get out our three major strategies for caring for the Earth community
9. (B) *Inner Council*: an exercise that allows one to meditate on who s/he really listens to in making big decisions in life[5]

Creation-Focused

10. (K) *Universe Walk*: using a long rope or a tract of land, mark the 13-15 billion-year universe journey through major turning points to rehearse the universe story

11. (D) *Ecozoic Circle*: describe how you would help bring a better human-Earth relationship to an ongoing group of eight or more persons

12. (B) *Creation Vigil*: each person is sent out to spend the night by herself/himself under the stars — a little away from all other persons and human-made distractions — to experience the depth and immensity of the universe journey

Now is the time for creating and experimenting with new spiritual exercises that remind us that we are spiritual and that we are taking a leap toward creation-centeredness.

Spirit as Intensification

As human beings we have experiences of body, experiences of mind, and the intensification of each is the experience of Spirit.

Experiences of body include, for example, sensations, feelings, emotions, breath, intimacy, expenditure, work, sport, pain, fear, crises, death. Experiences of body that became for me experiences of Spirit have been funeral services of my cats as a boy, falling in love, air flight into Kathmandu, holding my two sons and two grandchildren at birth, holding on as Hurricane Hugo blasted my hometown, leaving my secular-religious Order, many years later reuniting with over three-hundred old colleagues at our global Order reunion, the murder and suicide of a couple I counseled and married, the last rites for my mother. (List your own experiences of body and be sensitive to your state of being.)

Experiences of mind include, for example, thoughts, perceptions, conceptions, judgments, values, dreams, entertainment, beauty, contingency, wonder, otherness, limits, adoration, relationships, sacramental universe, sympathy, compassion, despair, gratitude. Experiences of mind that became for me experiences of Spirit have been seeing my Earth home on TV (1969), reading the *Courage To Be*, identifying with the doom of oppressed villagers, reading that over 100 million have been killed in wars of the 20th century, recently learning that 450 humans own more than half of the planet's assets, meditative consciousness while writing. (List your own experiences of mind and be sensitive to your state of being.)

Calling to memory such experiences of the spirit journey is another way to make conscious one's life with Spirit. With that consciousness comes a state of being or special awareness that fills the moment, upon reflection. In Reflections 6 through 10 we referred to *The Other World Charts*, which is a construct with 144 states of being we experience under the categories of mystery, consciousness, care, and fulfillment. That chart is simply another tool for making us aware of our experiences that signify our relationship with Spirit. We also described the *big feel*, the *big think*, and the *big resolve* as the way we naturally reflect upon our experiences.

In Reflection 6 we described another helpful reflection method called the *art form conversation*. Its deepening four levels of questions guide persons or groups in their reflections upon a particular art form, such as a movie, or upon anything from reflecting on a year in one's life at a birthday party to reflecting on what's been happening in the world since September 11. This method is another practical spiritual tool following our natural reflection patterns.

Through the natural reflection process we can keep in touch with Spirit. Our relationship with Spirit is a natural affair as we converse, drive to work, go to sleep, wonder as we wander throughout our lives, ruminating with the facility of conscious reflection. We obviously *are* spiritual beings.

Practical Signs of the Spiritual Revolution

My friend John Patterson, a manager in a successful company in Hong Kong, suggests that if we did only one spiritual exercise daily it would have three parts: to immerse ourselves in wonder daily; list five specifics we are thankful for daily; and symbolize and enact our concern for others daily. Then, a consciousness of the blessing that life always is would abound in us and be seen by others through us. I think John has put his finger on something: a simple way to rehearse the goodness of life (because Spirit is present), a daily discipline of being thankful, and a daily way to remind ourselves that our spirit journey is about care for others, creation. Maybe it's a simple trilogy of 1) life is good, 2) yeah! 3) and why not pass it on?[6]

Sam Keen has rich practical suggestions about communing with Spirit:

> Set aside regular times for meditative thinking, recollection, and silence. As a practical matter, it is good to rise early enough to set the tone of your upcoming day by enjoying leisurely moments — a graceful caress, a ritual shower of purification, a consecrated breakfast, a conversation about what matters with family or friend. Practice or omit whatever formal rituals you like — meditation, prayer, tai chi, chanting, reading of texts — that will remind you to enter the day with a spirit of gratitude and devotion.[7]

People all over the globe, from John to Sam to Oprah to Ken Wilber, are beginning to create rituals and practices for practicing the presence of the always already present Spirit, because as we said in Reflection 1, there is a spiritual revolution going on, with no high priests but a planetary priesthood of all believers. This revolution is taking shape through individual religious practices in church or mosque; it is also taking place in the workplace and school in appropriate ways, and in the home.

I am reminded of a movie where children stared wide-eyed as their grandfather reverently lit the candles of the Hanukkah menorah and told the powerful story of their tribe. I asked myself What is the equivalent today for the major celebrations in our homes that will deliver the fundamental truths of Spirit? If not the TV, what will be the new spirit mode for our western culture, especially, that is more absorbed in entertainment than in intentional reflection?

Closing Exercises

To prove we can creatively tune in to Spirit any which way, anywhere, and anytime we choose, let us consider last rites in a creation-centered context and then some novel design for our vocational intent:

> When Chuang Tzu was about to die, his disciples began planning a splendid funeral.
> But he said: 'I shall have heaven and earth for my coffin; the sun and moon will be the jade symbols hanging by my side; planets and constellations will shine as jewels all around me, and all beings will be present as mourners at the wake. What more is needed? Everything is amply taken care of! . . .'[8]

Why not take some time in the near future to consider how you want to be put away. This can be a revealing spiritual exercise. I wrote eight pages about my last rites in my memoir, and rereading them helps me see through the fog in my living.

Likewise, play around with a graphic way to represent what your life is about. Practical spiritual exercises can be intriguing and fun as well as edifying, releasing us to become secular monks and nuns on the run.

We *are* spiritual beings, created to . . .

*

* * *

*

To *see*
To *care*
To *be* aware
To *live* simply
To *love* creation
To *work* on behalf of
To *celebrate* our living
To *reflect* on the awesome
To *serve* the shattered Earth
To *dream* the impossible dream
To *home* on Earth as one community

=
=

Exercise: 200+ Nations – Family Intercession

Let us read[1] the names of most of our Earth's nations — more than two hundred — just to remind ourselves of the habitat of our Earth family, imaging all in our care and all in the fellowship of our planetary responsibility. It is good if we as a family know each other's names, so we can more and more keep each other in mind:

Afghanistan, Albania, Algeria, Andorra, Angola, Antigua and Barbuda, Argentina, Armenia, Australia, Austria, Azerbaijan, Bahamas, Bahrain, Bangladesh, Barbados, Belarus, Belgium, Belize, Benin, Bermuda, Bhutan, Bolivia, Botswana, Brazil, British Virgin Islands, Brunei Darussalam, Bulgaria, Burkina Faso, Burundi, Cambodia, Cameroon, Canada, Cape Verde, Central African Republic, Chad, Chile, China, Colombia, Comoros, Congo, Costa Rica, Côte d'Ivoire, Croatia, Cuba, Cyprus, Czech Republic, Democratic People's Republic of Korea, Democratic Republic of the Congo, Denmark, Djibouti, Dominica, Dominican Republic, Ecuador, Egypt, El Salvador, Equatorial Guinea, Eritrea, Estonia, Ethiopia, Falkland Islands, Federal Republic of Yugoslavia, Federated States of Micronesia, Fiji, Finland, France, French Guiana, French Polynesia, Gabon, Gambia, Georgia, Germany, Ghana, Gibraltar, Greece, Greenland, Grenada, Guam, Guatemala, Guinea, Guinea-Bissau, Guyana, Haiti, Honduras, Hungary, Iceland, India, Indonesia, Iraq, Ireland, Islamic Republic of Iran, Islands of the Caribbean, Islands of the Pacific, Israel, Italy, Jamaica, Japan, Jordan, Kazakhstan, Kenya, Kiribati, Kuwait, Kyrgyzstan, Lao People's Democratic Republic,

Latvia, Lebanon, Lesotho, Liberia, Libyan Arab Jamahiriya, Liechtenstein, Lithuania, Luxembourg, Macau, Macedonia, Madagascar, Malawi, Malaysia, Maldives, Mali, Malta, Marshall Islands, Mauritania, Mauritius, Mayotte, Mexico, Monaco, Mongolia, Morocco, Mozambique, Myanmar, Namibia, Nauru, Nepal, Netherlands, New Caledonia, New Zealand, Nicaragua, Niger, Nigeria, North Korea, Norway, Oman, Pakistan, Palau, Panama, Papua New Guinea, Paraguay, Peru, Philippines, Poland, Portugal, Puerto Rico, Qatar, Republic of Bosnia and Herzegovina, Republic of Moldova, Romania, Russian Federation, Rwanda, Saint Kitts and Nevis, Saint Lucia, Saint Vincent and the Grenadines, Samoa, San Marino, Sao Tome and Principe, Saudi Arabia, Senegal, Seychelles, Sierra Leone, Singapore, Slovakia, Slovenia, Solomon Islands, Somalia, South Africa, South Korea, Spain, Sri Lanka, Sudan, Suriname, Swaziland, Sweden, Switzerland, Syrian Arab Republic, Taiwan, Tajikistan, Tanzania, Thailand, The former Yugoslav Republic of Macedonia, Togo, Tonga, Trinidad and Tobago, Tunisia, Turkey, Turkmenistan, Tuvalu,[2] Uganda, Ukraine, United Arab Emirates, United Kingdom of Great Britain and Northern Ireland, United Republic of Tanzania, United States of America, Uruguay, Uzbekistan, Vanuatu, Venezuela, Viet Nam, Western Sahara, Yemen, Zambia, and Zimbabwe.

These are the nations of our extended family of human beings and natural habitats. They all are in the union of our care.

---

[1] One can go to Merriam-Webster Online (www.m-w.com) to hear any one of the names pronounced. Wouldn't hurt to recite the names ritualistically like a good pastor calls the names of his/her parishioners at the altar regularly or a good President regularly calls the roll of the places where her people live.
[2] Going out of being because of recent rising ocean due to global warming.

I Bow to Spirit: Namaste

Through you
I bow to Spirit.
Namaste.

Whether you believe the "trinity,"
or "Spirit" as the name for all three,
you believe It is,
from the beginning till now,
creating, recreating.
Namaste.

Spirit works Its own way
everyday through events,
spoken, written, or imaged word;
through any part of creation,
through any person,
or through a vision:
Spirit truths and lifes us.
Namaste.

Spirit is breath and non-,
height and depth,
edge and center,
beginning and end,
non-being in being.
Namaste.

Born of Spirit.
In Spirit we live, move,
and have our being.
Blessed be we by Spirit.
Namaste.

So bow to all others in Its name,
Its children all.
Namaste.

—11/14/2000 kec's 5th birthday

Epilogue:
Spirit Is That Without Which

What is needed is closer to the conversion process of the
great religious transformations. . . . [Let us] begin a new
phase of existence in our own lives . . . with a primacy of
appreciation for what the natural world tells us: I will feed
you, I will clothe you, I will shelter you, I will heal you;
only do not *use* me in a way that degrades me, a way that
prevents me from awakening in you those wonderful inner
qualities of wonder, beauty and intimacy.[1]

~Thomas Berry

Creation is transparent to Spirit, therefore,
>Creation awes us
>Creation communes with us
>Creation sustains us
>Creation transforms us

Spirit is the prime mover
>Moving only in creation
>>— as far as we know —
>Our primal community

~jpc

THAT WITHOUT WHICH we will not make it into the future:

- creation values over human values
- communion among earthlings
- a new spirit mode

Therefore, three things must happen to change our world:
1) *creation-centeredness*, releasing us humans to repent for and be
reconciled with the oppressed and enslaved parts of creation: for

219

example, air, water, land, forests, plants, animals, humans; 2) *holistic belief,* releasing us humans from our divisive belief systems of fundamentalism, tribalism, capitalism, and nationalism that we defend with military and terrorist brutality; and 3) a *new social vehicle* that is built on the *new spirit mode* of intercommunion, releasing us six billion humans to care for all Earth forms through comprehensive economic, political, and cultural structures.

All this is the context for our great work. Practically, this would mean that Ecozoic pioneers bringing to be the Ecozoic Era be able to answer from the heart the knowing, doing, and being questions that will make all the difference:

- How do we come to understand that the everyday happenings, encounters, and dialogue of creation are transparent to Spirit?
- How do we communicate that we are "willed for a life of communion"?[2]
- How do we embody our 100 percent freedom responsibly on behalf of all?
- As Spirit sustains, awakens, forms, engages, and unites, how do we remold human training around these profound human journey dynamics?
- Or how do we motivate and sustain humans within the *great work movement* of service?

Without answers to these questions, creation pioneers will not be effective. Our Earth community will not recover until we humans profoundly change our ways.

The "conversion process" that "is needed" — to use Berry's words from the opening quote — is the transformation of our human images that devolve Earth and retard its holistic re-creation. That which lies in the wake of our human waves of bigotry, arrogance, and a complex of superiority must be wary until human conversion happens. Besides our human lynchings, apartheid, racial cleansings, holocausts, and wars, how in the name of all that is holy can we abide "biocide" (the murder of nature) and "geocide"[3] (the murder of the Earth), which are not much on our prayer lists, because till now they have not shown up much on our screens of consciousness? Truly, besides the "personal self," the "family [and tribal] self," there is the "Earth self" and the "universe self."[4] We are waking up to "they are all one self." Human development only makes sense *within* the context of creation development. I believe we are beginning to understand that *creation development* "transcends and includes" human development.

The depth dimension is the key to life, ecology, civilization, and is our biggest challenge.[5] Throughout this book we have been saying that unless we see through to the spirit dimension of existence, there will be no significant change in our endeavors, be they economic, political, cultural, or ecological. How do we get out of flatland and into the spirit domain of creation-centered living?

What are some profound things we can do to symbolize our conversion? What about rewriting our constitutions to include nonhuman rights? What about using our taxes to pay at least as much for care of earthlings as military defense? What about funding programs for Earth literacy at least as well as language literacy? (I won't even mention reducing car and light-truck emissions to zero.) What about Earth-care awards becoming at least as significant as peace and movie awards? Or what about changing the word "humanities" to a more inclusive word in higher education? What about a new identity — like Patrick Henry saying, after the American Revolution, "I am no longer a Virginian but an American"? What about our saying, "I am no longer human-centered but creation-centered"? And what about learning to see through creation to its deep unity, its deep wonder, its deep fulfillment?

We humans may at last pick up our destiny:

not as the center of creation,
neither as victims to the immensity of creation,
but as sacrificial servants of creation.

What is bringing about this conversion in us humans is Spirit's gift of consciousness: we have a spiritual sensitivity to the heart of existence, to communion with Spirit. Growing out of that dialogue comes our spiritual responsibility for the future evolution of our beloved planet and its atmosphere.

Spirit is that without which this transformation will not happen. Spirit helps us to descend, to experience the hell that other species and humans are trying to live through; and It helps us to transcend our myopia of being human so that we be freed to live on behalf of creation.

Spirit would be at one with us, communing with us and motivating our responses to live on behalf of. That's what Spirit does, fulfilling us in the process. We are led by That which surely reigns and are called to respond on behalf of Its whole kingdom.

Finally, Spirit is that without which our lives and creation will not be fulfilled. This is my witness.

Not I, not I, but the wind that blows through me!
A fine wind is blowing the new direction of Time.
If only I let it bear me, carry me, if only it carry me!
If only I am sensitive, subtle, oh, delicate, a winged gift!
If only, most lovely of all, I yield myself and am borrowed
By the fine, fine wind that takes its course through the
        chaos of the world
Like a fine, an exquisite chisel, a wedge-blade inserted;
If only I am keen and hard like the sheer tip of a wedge
Driven by invisible blows,
The rock will split, we shall come at the wonder, we shall
        find the Hesperides. . . .[6]

~D. H. Lawrence

Verse 34

Spiritually Evolved?

As we evolve do we get better?
Are molecules better than atoms?
Or multicellular better than cellular?
Or bigger-brained better than smaller-?

Are things better than ever?
What about the tens of million humans
and thousands of species
we killed during the 20th century?
Which century is more evolved,
the last one or the first of the first millennium?

What does evolution have to do with Spirit?
Does Spirit evolve?
Do the evolved become more spiritual?
How can anything be any closer
to Spirit than anything else,
regardless of time and space?

Who is more enlightened?
is a different question.
Can a group of humans
come together and care
> for the masses,
> the biosphere,
> the geosphere,
> and the atmosphere?

If so, are they more evolved?
Yes.

More aware of Spirit's presence?
Most likely.

Any closer to Spirit?
How can they be?

Any better?
Of course not,
for Spirit is impartial
(or absolutely partial
to everything).

—*september 2001*

225

Appendix

My Response to Bishop Spong's *"Twelve Theses: A Call for a New Reformation"*[1]

[I was struck by his theses and wish to dialogue with them using "Spirit" language. I ask the reader to enter the dialogue by answering the ten questions at the end. My reflections are below each of Spong's numbered and bold statements. ~jpc]

1. **Theism, as a way of defining God, is dead. God can no longer be understood with credibility as a Being, supernatural in power, dwelling above the sky and prepared to invade human history periodically to enforce the divine will. So, most theological God-talk today is meaningless unless we find a new way to speak of God.**

"God is Spirit" is one way to move. Spirit is less an object and more of a force, power, energy that brings us to deeper awareness.

2. **Since God can no longer be conceived in theistic terms, it becomes nonsensical to seek to understand Jesus as the incarnation of the theistic deity. So, the Christology of the ages is bankrupt.**

The Trinity is an image, not a reality. Jesus is the historical man who has become transparent to life lived in the Spirit, through his freedom, faith, and passion. "Jesus the man" and "Christ the event" are both historical, but Christ the event is more historical, touching our life experience. The experienced reality of a transformative power in our lives is the point of Christology.

3. **The biblical story of the perfect and finished creation from which human beings fell into sin is pre-Darwinian mythology and post-Darwinian nonsense.**

Creation is always in process of transformation in response to the power of Spirit that makes life the way it is — always in response.

4. **The virgin birth, understood as literal biology, makes the divinity of Christ, as traditionally understood, impossible.**

St. John demythologizes the virgin birth: we are all born of a virgin, all children of the Spirit. Let us deliteralize the scriptures and live their message of truth. Maybe literal truth is an illusion.

5. **The miracle stories of the New Testament can no longer be interpreted in a post-Newtonian world as supernatural events performed by an incarnate deity.**

All have been brought back to life like Lazarus, in small ways, at least. Life in the Spirit is rather miraculous in ordinary ways. The New Testament is not about magic. If it were, faith would not be its theme.

6. **The view of the cross as the sacrifice for the sins of the world is a barbarian idea based on primitive concepts of God that must be dismissed.**

This medieval concept of atonement for sin does not make any sense when seen in the light of "original blessing." So, at-one-ment is reawakenment to life in the Spirit, being reunited to that from which we have been estranged.

7. **Resurrection is an action of God, who raised Jesus into the meaning of God. It therefore cannot be a physical resuscitation occurring inside human history (pg. 454 ff.).**

Creation is resurrectional. Life is resurrectional. Resurrection takes place in history because the Spirit is in history. We do not know whether Spirit is beyond history, but we believe Spirit is eternal because it is at the heart of history.

8. **The story of the ascension assumed a three-tiered universe and is therefore not capable of being translated into the concepts of a post-Copernican space age.**

The three-storied universe of the 1st century is not our worldview. Yet, we can understand their urge to try to communicate the trans-historical and primordial dimension of Spirit. Reality was not flat for them as it seems to be for us.

9. **There is no external, objective, revealed standard writ in Scripture or on tablets of stone that will govern our ethical behavior for all time.**

Scripture is no authority for anything unless it is scripture's message that our authority is in our free response to Spirit on behalf of creation. This means each of us finally decides where s/he stands and what s/he lives out of and on behalf of.

10. **Prayer cannot be a request made to a theistic deity to act in human history in a particular way.**

Prayer is intercommunion with Spirit and creation.

11. **The hope for life after death must be separated forever from the behavior-control mentality of reward and punishment. The church must abandon, therefore, its reliance on guilt as a motivator of behavior.**

Our motivation is from our intercommunion with eternal Spirit. We are eternal as we are one with Spirit, which never goes out of being.

12. **All human beings bear God's image and must be respected for what each person is. Therefore, no external description of one's being, whether based on race, ethnicity, gender, or sexual orientation, can properly be used as the basis for either rejection or discrimination.**

Spirit is not made in our image. Each piece of creation is sacred, touched by Spirit, transparent to Spirit. Equality of creation — not just "all men are created equal" — is our radical declaration of interdependence.

Spong's Note: "These theses posted for debate are inevitably stated in a negative manner. That is deliberate. Before one can hear what Christianity is one must create room for that hearing by clearing out the misconceptions of what Christianity is not."

My Note: What if we were to enlarge upon the mission of Jesus and all religions. I have trouble with a mission statement that leaves out creation and seems to focus mostly on humans experiencing God. I've heard the line before that care for creation will follow. I don't see Christianity nor the Eastern religious, who are intent upon "experiencing Being," as deeply caring for the Earth — yet. Maybe something is wrong with the formula.

230

What about putting the first and second commandments together again, as did Jesus, who moved beyond spiritualism (just love of God) and humanism (just love of the neighbor). The only thing that's changed is the vastness of the neighbor: no longer just a person next door but an Earth community (including six billion humans) and environment that are deteriorating extremely fast.

The debate within and among all religions needs a new focus. I was struck by thirteen religious traditions' statements of the Golden Rule on a poster presented to the UN and now displayed there.[2] As I read them, only the Aboriginal, Jain, and Unitarian statements of the golden rule include a more comprehensive "other" than the human. "Do unto others as you would have them do unto you" is about *all* others, not just humans. How do we focus humanity beyond human salvation, or on the rest of creation?

This is where I wish Spong, the Jesus Seminar, and others would push Christianity, beyond human-centeredness, else it will surely die. A right-relationship with a god made in "man's image" is not saving the church, religions, nor the Earth community. At least that's my observation.

---

[1] By John S. Spong, *Here I Stand: My Struggle for a Christianity of Integrity, Love, and Equality* (San Francisco: Harper, 2000), pp. 453-4; drawn from his book *Why Christianity Must Change or Die: A Bishop Speaks to Believers in Exile.*
[2] "Golden Rules For a Culture of Peace," presented to Mrs. Gillian Sorensen, Assistant Secretary-General of the United Nations, on January 4, 2002. Read the article: http://www.templeofunderstanding.org/temple_news_m.htm

Reflection

1. I <u>circle</u> one of the 12 theses of Bishop Spong or one of author's comments that is most on target.
2. I <u>check</u> one I would like to question.
3. What is my felt (not intellectual) response to this appendix dialogue?

4. Looking at my circled one (#1), why is it on target?

5. Looking at my checked one (#2), what is my question?

6. What do the final three paragraphs ("My Note") have to do with my spirit journey?

7. What do I think should be the focus of a person's spirit journey?

8. What person or persons would I hope would take these pages seriously?

9. What will "save" the church, religions, and the Earth community?

10. What is my role in said "salvation" process?

NOTES

New Context

[1] "Only after the bombs of Hiroshima and Nagasaki did humans begin to recognize the possibility that they could destroy the planet by their own expropriated power." Rosemary Ruether, *Gaia and God: An Ecofeminist Theology of Earth Healing* (San Francisco: Harper, 1992), p. 206.

[2] Adapted from *Building the Earth*, p. vii. Originally from *Spirit of Earth* (1931), p. 37.

[3] Institute of Cultural Affairs ritual used with community projects around the world.

PROLOGUE: Where I'm Coming From

[1] I will refer to these two as "the Institutes" throughout the book. The Institute of Cultural Affairs (ICA) now does methods facilitation and training, consultations, and community projects around the world.

[2] Huston Smith, *The Illustrated World's Religions: A Guide to Our Wisdom Tradition* (San Francisco: Harper, 1994), pp. 40-1.

[3] A. L. Basham, *The Origins and Development of Classical Hinduism,* ed. Kenneth G. Zysk, (Boston: Beacon, 1989), pp. 10-11.

[4] Ursala Goodenough, a molecular biologist, is part of my audience, I hope. Interviewed by Mary Lacombe, "Emergent Wonder: The Sacred Depths of Nature," on *Science and Spirit* Web site www.science-spirit.com, she says, "I regard myself as a religious non-theist, meaning that God questions are not central to my quest and, indeed, get in the way of it." And I appreciate what she says next, "But I am deeply informed and moved by the texts and the art of traditional and indigenous

religions, and I believe they offer us much guidance and wisdom as we chart our paths." She states well the tension of not using and using God-talk.

[5] *The Saviors of God,* trans. Kimon Friar (New York: Simon and Schuster, 1960), p. 95.

[6] Ibid., p. 100.

[7] "When All Thoughts," Ryokan, trans. John Stevens, *Dewdrops on a Lotus Leaf: Zen Poems of Ryokan* (Boston: Shambhala, 1995), p. 20.

REFLECTION 1: Spiritual Revolution

[1] *One River, Many Wells* (New York: Thatcher/Putnam, 2000), pp. 6-8. The quotes from the Dalai Lama come from his *Ethics for the New Millennium* (New York: Riverhead, 1999).

[2] *The Shattered Spectrum: A Survey of Contemporary Theology* (Atlanta: John Knox, 1981), p. 205.

[3] George Gallup, Jr., *Surveying the Religious Landscape*, (Harrisburg, Penn.: Morehouse, 1999).

[4] *World Christian Encyclopedia*, 2001 edition.

[5] "Faith Communities in the United States Today," by Bill Broadway, *Washington Post*, March 13, 2001.

[6] Wade Clark Roof, *A Generation of Seekers: The Spiritual Journeys of the Baby Boom Generation* (San Francisco: Harper, 1993), quoted in Robert D. Putnam's *Bowling Alone: The Collapse and Revival of American Community* (New York: Simon & Schuster, 2000), p. 73.

[7] "Poll Shows Protestant Collapse," by Uwe Siemon-Netto, United Press International, June 28, 2001.

[8] P. 300.

[9] *Fortune.com*, Marc Gunther, "God and Business: The Surprising Quest for Spiritual Renewal in the American Workplace," p. 1 (from *Fortune Magazine*, July 9, 2001).

[10] Paraphrase of Cupitt's talk given at the Spring 2001 Jesus Seminar gathering at Westar Institute in California.

[11] Brian Swimme in his Foreword to Teilhard's *The Human Phenomenon*, p. xv. Here he is recounting how Berry counseled him during their time together at Riverside Research Center in New York.

[12] "Religion and Ecology: The Interaction of Cosmology and Cultivation," *The Good in Nature and Humanity: Connecting Science, Religion, and Spirituality with the Natural World*, ed. Stephen R. Kellert and Timothy J. Farnham (Washington, DC: Island, 2002), p. 67.

[13] *Science and Religion* (New York: Random House, 1987), p. 335.

[14] *The Human Phenomenon* (the acclaimed new English translation, after forty years, of *The Phenomenon of Man* — a mistranslation of the original title, *Le phénomène humain*), ed. and trans. Sarah Appleton-Weber (Brighton: Sussex Academic, 1999), p. 178.

[15] In conjunction with the Philadelphia Center for Religion and Science, Dr. William Grassie, Executive-Director; also editor of metanexus.net.

[16] "A quantum computer, by its very logical nature, is in principle capable of simulating the entire quantum universe in which it is embedded. . . . In other words, a small part of reality can in some sense capture and embody the whole. The fact that the physical universe is constructed in this way — that wholes and parts are mutually enfolded in mathematical self-consistency — is a stunning discovery that impacts on philosophy and even theology. By achieving quantum computation, mankind will lift a tiny corner of the veil of mystery that shrouds the ultimate nature of reality. We shall finally have captured the vision elucidated so eloquently by William Blake two centuries ago: 'To see a World in a grain of sand, And a Heaven in a wild flower, Hold infinity in the palm of your hand, And eternity in an hour.'" —Paul Davies, "Quantum Computing," Metaviews 022.2000.02.22, www.metanexus.net.

[17] Marc Gunther, *Fortune.com*, op. cit.

[18] Sharon Begley, with Anne Underwood, *Newsweek*, May 7, 2001, p. 50.

[19] "The challenges inherent in creating a Department of Peace are massive," said Congressman Kucinich from Ohio, July 11, 2001. "But the alternatives are worse. Violence at home, in the schools, in the media, and between nations has dragged down humanity. It's time to recognize that traditional, militant objectives for peace are not working, and the only solution is to make peace the goal of a cabinet level agency."

[20] *What Is Enlightenment* magazine, Spring/Summer 2001, pp. 28-9.

[21] Parker J. Palmer, printed in *The Weavings Reader: Living with God in the World*, ed. John Mogabgab (Nashville: The Upper Room, 1993), p. 183.

236

REFLECTION 2: Our One Spirit Tradition

[1] Pierre Teilhard de Chardin, *Activation of Energy* (London: Harcourt Brace Jovanovich, 1970), p. 238. Dr. William (Billy) Grassie introduced me to this quote at a two-day seminar at Timberlake Farm near Burlington, North Carolina, where he dialogued with Thomas Berry, also one of his mentors.
[2] His *The Human Phenomenon* (new translation of *The Phenomenon of Man*), *The Divine Milieu*, *The Future of Man*, *Hymn of the Universe*, *Building the Earth*, and others, were printed posthumously.

REFLECTION 3: A Hundred Ways

[1] Thomas Berry, *The Dream of the Earth*, p. 135.
[2] Here I refer to "soul" as one's interiority. I hardly use the word "soul" in this book. I like what Gene W. Marshall says about "soul": "My conclusion is that the term 'soul' is not needed any more. It might be used to mean the same thing as 'Spirit.' It might be used to mean some aspect of our finite personalities, but in that case other terms are less confusing. Perhaps the word 'soul' can be a general term for the entire interior life. But in my religious thinking, I am going to view the word 'soul' as an obsolete substantialistic term used in times past to point to the dynamics of 'Spirit.'" From "Some Basic Definitions," Discourse 1, *The Stages of Consciousness and the Experience of Spirit* (Bonham, TX: Realistic Living, 2000).
[3] There is no scientific consensus here, but it's trending back in time.
[4] Are Spirit and creation one? My experience says *No*. I can say I am in Spirit and Spirit is in me, but I refrain. Spirit permeates my existence but is really not me. I am more comfortable sticking with *I-Thou* instead of *I-I*. Maybe there is an in-between, but I doubt it.

REFLECTION 4: Spirituality

[1] These couplets are adapted from my *Motivation for the Great Work*, pp. xxvi-xxvii.
[2] Alicia S. Carpenter, "Just as Long as I Have Breath," 1981, from *Singing the Living Tradition*, songbook of The Unitarian Universalist

Association, 1993, song number 6.

[3] "Are You Looking for Me?" (25), *The Kabir Book*: *Forty-four of the Ecstatic Poems of Kabir*, trans. versions by Robert Bly (Boston: Beacon, 1977), p. 33.

[4] Figure 1, "The Great Nest of Being" chart, *Integral Psychology* (Boston: Shambhala, 2000), p. 6.

[5] *Ken Wilber Online*, "On the Nature of a Post-Metaphysical Spirituality: Response to Habermas and Weis" (Part I).

[6] W. H. Werkmeister, *Nicolai Hartmann's New Ontology* (Tallahassee: Florida State University Press, 1990), pp. 157-68.

[7] *The Marriage of Sense and Soul* (New York: Random House, 1998), p. 196.

[8] "We Are Transmitters," *The Complete Poems of D. H. Lawrence* (New York: Penguin, 1977), p. 449.

[9] "A Spirituality that Transforms," *One Taste*: *Daily Reflections on Integral Spirituality* (Boston: Shambhala, 2000), p. 33-4.

REFLECTION 6: Transparency

[1] *Human Energy* (New York: Harcourt Brace Jovanovich, 1969), p. 130.

[2] *The Saviors of God*, p. 84.

[3] "Toward a New Other-Worldliness," *Theology Today*, April 1944, Vol. 1, No. 1, pp. 78-87 [italics added]. (The phrase "the other world in this world" appears chronologically later in poems and prose by David Whyte, Max Reif, Stephen King.)

[4] "The Other World," presented at EI/ICA Summer Program, July 1972, Chicago (unpublished).

[5] Quoted from an unpublished essay by Mrs. R. F. Sasaki in Huston Smith's *The Religions of Man* (New York: Harper, 1958), p. 152.

[6] *The Sickness Unto Death*, trans. Walter Lowrie, p. 19. We will discuss Kierkegaard's Spirit formula in Reflection 8.

[7] Mathews' *The Christ of History* in my *The Transparent Event, p.* 113. For a more in-depth understanding of Joseph W. Mathews' thought, read Chapters 12-14 of *The Transparent Event*: *Postmodern Christ Images.*

[8] George Weiss and Bob Thiele, Harold Square Music, on behalf of Range Road Music and Quartet Music (ASCAP).

[9] *Gaia & God* (San Francisco: Harper, 1991), p. 139.

[10] *The Human Phenomenon*, p. 6.

[11] Ibid., p. 24-6.

[12] Throughout his *Hymn of the Universe* (New York: Harper & Row, 1961).
[13] Paul Tillich, *Biblical Religion and the Search for Ultimate Reality* (Chicago: University of Chicago, 1955), pp. 22-3.
[14] *I and Thou* (Smith), p. 75.
[15] Method of the Order: Ecumenical/ Ecumenical Institute/ Institute of Cultural Affairs. See the book Brian Stanfield edited, *The Art of Focused Conversation*.
[16] *The Human Phenomenon*, p. 3 (italics added).
[17] *From the Heart* article by Alan Cohen at http://www.alancohen.com/html/may2001.html: "The True Perfectionist," May 2001.

REFLECTION 7: Spirit Comes as Wonder

[1] *The Idea of the Holy*, Chap. IV, pp. 12-13, and Chap. VI, pp. 31-8.
[2] *The Shaking of the Foundations*, p. 162.
[3] "Acceptance is as important to social animals as oxygen and food." Howard Bloom, *Global Brain*, Chapter 9, http://www.heise.de/tp/english/special/glob/default.html.
[4] P. 176.
[5] *Systematic Theology* III (Chicago: University of Chicago, 1963), pp. 111-12.
[6] *C. G. Jung Letters*, Vol I (1906-1950), ed. Gerhard Adler, Aniela Jaffe, and R.F.C. Hull (Princeton: Princeton, 1973), letter to P. W. Martin, p. 377.

REFLECTION 8: Spirit Comes as Freedom

[1] This quote is a mixture from Buber's *I and Thou* translations by Ronald Gregor Smith, pp. 76-8, and by Walter Kaufmann, pp. 124-6.
[2] The charts of the Order: Ecumenical/ Institute of Cultural Affairs/ Ecumenical Institute are in print in Brian Stanfield's book, *The Courage to Lead* (Gabriola Island, Canada: New Society, 2000), pp. 106-13.
[3] "The Other World," July 1972 (unpublished).
[4] Kierkegaard, *Concluding Unscientific Postscript*, ed. Walter Lowrie (Princeton: Princeton, 1941), p. 182.
[5] *I and Thou*, trans. Ronald Gregor Smith, p. 86; trans. Walter Kaufmann, p. 134.

[6] Kierkegaard, *Fear and Trembling* and *The Sickness Unto Death*, trans. Walter Lowrie (New York: Doubleday, 1954), p. 147. In this translation, "posited" and "constituted" are used interchangeably, but "constituted" is used more.

[7] *The Stages of Consciousness and the Experience of Spirit* , p. 16.

[8] Einstein's story from Brian Swimme, *The Hidden Heart of the Cosmos*: *Humanity and the New Story* (Maryknoll, NY: Orbis, 1996), pp. 70-4.

[9] *Religion in an Age of Science* (San Francisco: Harper, 1990), p. 256.

[10] From O:E and Institutes' song "Free Am I," *The Singing of Those Who Care* (1980-81), p. 16, to the tune of "Summertime," by Gershwin-DuBose.

[11] *The Singing of Those Who Care* (1980-81), p. 157.

REFLECTION 9: Spirit Comes as Care

[1] From his dramatic poem *A Sleep of Prisoners* (Oxford: Oxford, 1951).

[2] *The Saviors of God*, p. 65.

[3] Ibid., p. 72.

[4] Martin Buber, *Moses* (New York: Harper, 1958), p. 164.

[5] Ibid.

[6] Excerpt from the Order: Ecumenical and the Institutes' songbook "The Singing of Those Who Care" (1980-81), p. 105, sung to the tune "Send In the Clowns," from *A Little Night Music* by Stephen Sondheim.

REFLECTION 10: Spirit Comes as Fulfillment

[1] *Journey to Ixtlan* (New York: Simon and Schuster, 1972), p.110.

[2] *The Saviors of God*, p. 58.

[3] Ibid., p. 79.

[4] Joseph Slicker, from his unpublished presentation "The Eternal Life," on The Other World Trek XVI, Summer 1972 conference in Chicago of The Institute of Cultural Affairs/The Ecumenical Institute: Chicago.

[5] *Hymns to an Unknown God*: *Awakening the Spirit in Everyday Life* (New York: Bantam, 1994), p. 266.

[6]*Putting on the Mind of Christ*: *The Inner Work of Christian Spirituality*, foreword by Ken Wilber (Charlottesville, Va.: Hampton Roads, 2000), pp. 3-4.

240

[7] Thomas Merton, *The Way of Chuang Tzu* (New York: New Directions, 1965), p. 27.
[8] Columbia Pictures, 1991. Director, Ron Underwood; Executive Producer, Billy Crystal.
[9] *Xaipe*, 65 (1950) from the *Selected Poems of E. E. Cummings* (New York: Liveright, 1994), p. 167 (punctuation his).
[10] Another translation, "How wonderful. All beings have this enlightened nature; only they have forgotten it."
[11] *The Stranger*, trans. Matthew Ward (New York: Vintage Books, 1988), p. 120.
[12] "The Myth of Sisyphus," *The Myth of Sisyphus and Other Essays*, trans. Justin O'Brien (New York: Vintage Books, 1991), p. 123.
[13] "Summer in Algiers," Ibid., p. 153.
[14] Slicker, op. cit.
[15] Nikos Kazantzakis, *Saint Francis* (New York: Simon and Schuster, 1962), pp. 95-6.
[16] Feodor Dostoevsky, *The Brothers Karamazov* (New York: Heritage, 1949), p. 280.

REFLECTION 11: Cosmological Revolution

[1] Center for Ecozoic Studies meeting, Greensboro, N.C., July 2001.
[2] *The Hidden Heart of the Cosmos*, pp. 61-2.
[3] *The Good in Nature and Humanity*, p. 76.
[4] Brian Swimme, interviewed by Renee Lertzman, "Experiencing Deep Time," *The Sun*, Issue 305, May 2001.
[5] *The Hidden Heart of the Cosmos*, p. 85.
[6] *Global Brain* (video), 1985.
[7] Interview of F. David Peat, "Look for Truth No Matter Where It Takes You," *WIE* magazine, Issue 11, 1998. (Peat was a colleague of Bohm and the writer of the biography, *Infinite Potential: The Life and Times of David Bohm*, November 1997.)
[8] Rosemary Ruether in her book *Gaia and God* thinks this phrase is unimaginative (p. 41). In *The Universe Story*, co-authors Swimme and Berry choose the imaginative name of "the primordial flaring forth."
[9] Bill Moyers, *The Power of Myth* (New York: Doubleday, 1988), pp. 72-7.
[10] *The New York Times Magazine*, April 15, 1979.

[11] These two good words have been spoken for by the Unitarian Universalists, the Quaker Universalists, and the Evangelical Universalists; and by counter-evolution groups such as the so-called Scientific Creationists, the American Indian Creationists, or the New Creationists — a pity, but best we not use the two words for talking about the cosmological revolution of our time.

[12] E-mail, April 9, 2002. Connie Barlow is the author of *Green Space, Green Time* (1997) and *The Ghosts of Evolution* (2001); Michael Dowd is author of *EarthSpirit: A Handbook for Nurturing Ecological Christianity* (1991). Together they are beginning an extended teaching and speaking tour to share the great story of evolution across North America.

[13] Thomas Berry, *The Dream of the Earth*, pp. 221-2 (italics added).

[14] Thomas Berry, from a talk at the Epic of Evolution Conference in Chicago, November 1997.

REFLECTION 12: Great Work Movement

[1] At the Nobel Peace Prize Centennial Symposium, Oslo, Norway, December 7, 2001, celebrating the 100th anniversary of the Nobel Prize, one-hundred Nobel laureates issued a brief but dire warning: immediate environmental and social reform are the "profound dangers" facing the world (OTVNewswire).

[2] *Dream of the Earth*. The fuller quote: "[F]inally, a reversal has begun, and the reality and value of the interior subjective numinous aspect of the entire cosmic order is being appreciated as the basic condition in which the [universe] story makes any sense at all. . . . All our human affairs . . . have their meaning precisely insofar as they enhance this . . . subjective intercommunion within the total range of reality. . . ," pp. 135-6.

[3] *Thomas Berry and the New Cosmology*, pp. 107-8.

[4] "Spiritual in origin or force," *Merriam-Webster.*

[5] *Dream of the Earth*, p. 132: "[W]e are moving into a new mythic age; it is little wonder that a kind of mutation is taking place in the entire earth-human order."

[6] Thomas Berry, "The Spirituality of the Earth," unpublished essay.

[7] *The Great Work*, p. 148.

[8] Ibid., p. 7.
[9] Ibid., p. 10.
[10] Ibid., p. 60.
[11] Ibid., p. 1.
[12] "Environmentalism: Return to Eden or Ticket to Hell?" © 2001 American Policy Center ["Return to Eden or Ticket to Hell," from the Web site *Post It*, circa 1994].
[13] Berry and Swimme, *The Universe Story*, op. cit., pp. 14-5.
[14] This Reflection has material from the "Preface," "Engagement: The Great Work," "New Spirit Mode," and the "Epilogue" of my book *Motivation for the Great Work*.
[15] Adapted from my *Motivation for the Great Work*, p. 193.

REFLECTION 13: Profound Human Journey

[1] *One Taste*, p. 28, from a piece printed elsewhere as "Spirituality That Transforms." Wilber compares experiences that "translate" and experiences that "transform" and contends that most religions are about translation, not transformation. Though I deeply appreciate this piece and Wilber's work in general, I must admit he is focused on human spiritual development — not really operating within the integral context of care for the Earth, even if he did write a 831-page book on *Sex, Ecology, Spirituality: The Spirit of Evolution*. Persons like Teilhard de Chardin and Thomas Berry would wonder why he uses the word "integral" when he is mostly focused on human development.

[2] In the Order: Ecumenical and the Institutes we created similar dynamics in a pentagon design. See page 35, *Motivation for the Great Work*, my book from which portions of this Reflection come.

[3] "The Cosmology of Religions" (unpublished paper).

[4] These reflections on St. John of the Cross come from our work in the Order: Ecumenical and the Ecumenical Institute: Chicago, and are especially well articulated in two unpublished lectures by Joseph Mathews and David McCleskey. The two books of St. John are combined in the *The Dark Night of the Soul and the Living Flame of Love* (San Francisco: Harper, 1995).

[5] *One Taste*, p. 26.

[6] Ibid., pp. 33-4.

REFLECTION 14: Practical Spirituality

[1] "Always Already," *The Eye of Spirit*, pp. 281-96. I agree with Wilber's quotes. I struggle to go all the way with his mysticism, even though we share the same paradigm of Spirit's presence. I will say he has the most conceptual clarity on post-metaphysical spirituality, or spirituality-in-this-world, of any writer I know.

[2] Wilber's word, *One Taste*, p. 129.

[3] Wilber in *One Taste,* pp. 121-3, gives a sample of comprehensive (he calls them "integral") practices for the physical, emotional, mental, social, cultural, and spiritual according to his four quadrants.

[4] "Swamp Gravy" is a drama group/annual presentation enterprise in Colquitt, Georgia, USA, that created its community story using this type of method with citizens. The storytelling that became the drama has been a stimulus to the community's economic health and spirit. More info at http://www.swampgravy.com.

[5] See my *The Transparent Event*, pp. 206-7, for procedures for this exercise.

[6] I would highly recommend a book by my colleague Basil Sharp entitled *The Adventure of Being Human*: *A Guide to Living a Fuller Life* (Washington, D.C.: Integrated Life Architects, 2000). It is a *Yes* piece of reflective journey verse within the context of the cosmos.

[7] "Taking Your Time: Kairos and Chronos," *Hymns to an Unknown God*, p. 267.

[8] From "Chuang Tzu's Funeral" [*xxxii. 14.*], op. cit., p. 156.

EPILOGUE: Spirit Is That Without Which

[1] From Berry's foreword to my *Motivation for the Great Work*, p. xiv.

[2] Martin Buber, *Between Man and Man*, trans. Ronald Gregor Smith (Boston: Beacon, 1955), p. 14.

[3] *Thomas Berry and the New Cosmology*, ed. Anne Lonergan and Caroline Richards (Mystic, Conn.: Twenty-Third, 1991), p. 12.

[4] Thomas Berry, with Thomas Clarke, *Befriending the Earth*: *A Theology of Reconciliation Between Humans and the Earth*, ed. Stephen Dunn and Anne Lonergan (Mystic, Conn.: Twenty-Third Publications, 1987), p. 135.

[5] "[T]he way beyond ecological crisis lies in solving the crisis of meaning. . . . A truly deep spiritual ecology would acknowledge the depth dimension of reality, rather than maintaining that the material natural system — the "web-of-life" — exhausts the infinite dimensions of the divine." —Michael Zimmerman, "Heidegger and Wilber on the Limitations of Spiritual Deep Ecology," quoted in Wilber's *One Taste*, p. 87.

[6] "Song of a Man Who Has Come Through," *The Complete Poems of D. H. Lawrence*, op. cit., p. 250.

Selected Bibliography

Armstrong, Karen. *Buddha*. New York: Lipper/Viking Press, 2001.

Barbour, Ian. *Religion in an Age of Science*. San Franciso: Harper, 1990.

Berry, Thomas, with Thomas Clarke. *Befriending the Earth: A Theology of Reconciliation Between Humans and the Earth*, ed. Stephen Dunn and Anne Lonergan. Mystic, Conn.: Twenty-Third, 1992.

——. *The Dream of the Earth*. 1988; San Francisco: Sierra Club, 1990.

——. *The Great Work: Our Way Into the Future*. New York: Random House, 1999.

——. *Thomas Berry and the New Cosmology*, ed. Anne Lonergan and Caroline Richards. Mystic, Conn.: Twenty-Third, 1991.

——. (with Brian Swimme) *The Universe Story: From the Primordial Flaring Forth to the Ecozoic Era — A Celebration of the Unfolding of the Cosmos*. New York: HarperCollins, 1992.

Bloom, Howard. *The Global Brain: The Evolution of Mass Mind from the Big Bang to the 21st Century*. New York: John Wiley, 2000.

Bonhoeffer, Dietrich. *A Testament to Freedom: The Essential Writings of Dietrich Bonhoeffer*. San Francisco: Harper, 1995.

Boulding, Kenneth. *The Image: Knowledge in Life and Society*. Ann Arbor: University of Michigan, 1971.

Buber, Martin. *Between Man and Man*, trans. Ronald Gregor Smith. Boston: Beacon, 1955.

——. *I and Thou*, trans. R. G. Smith. New York: Scribners, 1958.

——. *I and Thou*, trans. Walter Kaufmann. New York: Scribners, 1970.

——. *Moses*. New York: Harper, 1958.

Camus, Albert. *A Happy Death*. New York: Vintage, 1972.

——. *The Myth of Sisyphus and Other Essays*, trans. Justin O'Brien. New York: Vintage, 1991.

——. *The Stranger*, trans. Matthew Ward. New York: Vintage, 1988.

Castaneda, Carlos. *Journey to Ixtlan*. New York: Simon & Schuster, 1972.

Cock, John P. *Called To Be*: *A Spirit Odyssey*. Greensboro, N.C.: tranScribe, 2000.

———. *Motivation for the Great Work*: *Forty Meaty Meditations for the Secular-Religious*. San Jose: Authors Choice, 2000.

———. *The Transparent Event*: *Post-modern Christ Images*. Greensboro, N.C.: tranScribe, 2001.

Cox, Harvey. *Fire from Heaven*: *The Rise of Pentecostal Spirituality and the Reshaping of Religion in the Twenty-first Century*. Reading, Mass.: Addison-Wesley, 1995.

Cupitt, Don. *Reforming Christianity*. Santa Rosa: Polebridge Press, 2001.

Cummings, E. E. *Selected Poems of E. E. Cummings*. New York: Liveright, 1994.

Dalai Lama. *Ethics for the New Millennium*. New York: Riverhead Books, 1999.

Dostoevsky, Feodor. *The Brothers Karamazov*. New York: Heritage, 1949.

Fox, Matthew. *One River, Many Wells*. New York: Thatcher/Putnam, 2000.

———. *The Reinvention of Work*. New York: HarperCollins, 1994.

Fry, Christopher. *A Sleep of Prisoners*. Oxford: Oxford, 1951.

Goodenough, Ursala. *The Sacred Depths of Nature*. New York: Oxford, 1998.

Jung, C. G. *C. G. Jung Letters* I (1906-1950), ed. Adler, Jaffe, and Hull. Princeton: Princeton, 1973.

Kabir. *The Kabir Book*: *Forty-four of the Ecstatic Poems of Kabir*, trans. Robert Bly. Boston: Beacon, 1977.

Kazantzakis, Nikos. *The Saviors of God*: *Spiritual Exercises,* trans. Kimon Friar. New York: Simon & Schuster, 1960.

———. *Saint Francis*. New York: Simon & Schuster, 1962.

Keen, Sam. *Hymns to an Unknown God*: *Awakening the Spirit in Everyday Life*. New York: Bantam, 1994.

Kellert, S. R., and Timothy, J. F., (editors), *The Good in Nature and Humanity*: *Connecting Science, Religion, and Spirituality with the Natural World*. Washington, DC: Island, 2002.

Kierkegaard, Søren. *Concluding Unscientific Postscript*, trans. Walter Lowrie. Princeton: Princeton, 1941.

———. *Fear and Trembling* and *The Sickness Unto Death*, trans. Walter Lowrie. New York: Doubleday, 1954.

Kliever, Lonnie D. *The Shattered Spectrum*: *A Survey of Contemporary*

Theology. Atlanta: John Knox, 1981.

Lawrence, D. H. *The Complete Poems of D. H. Lawrence*. New York: Penguin, 1977.

Lesser, Elizabeth. *The New American Spirituality*. New York: Random House, 1999.

Marion, Jim. *Putting on the Mind of Christ*: *The Inner Work of Christian Spirituality*. Charlottesville, Va.: Hampton Roads Publishing, 2000.

Marshall, Gene W. *The Stages of Consciousness and the Experience of Spirit*. Bonham, Tx.: Realistic Living, 2000.

Mathews, Joseph W. *The Christ of History*. Chicago: *I.E.*, 1969.

Merton, Thomas. *The Way of Chuang Tzu*. New York: New Directions, 1965.

Niebuhr, H. Richard. "Toward a New Other-Worldliness," *Theology Today*, April 1944, Vol. 1, No. 1.

Otto, Rudolf. *The Idea of the Holy*. New York: Galaxy, 1958.

Putnam, Robert D. *Bowling Alone*: *The Collapse and Revival of American Community*. New York: Simon & Schuster, 2000.

Ralston, Holmes. *Science and Religion*: *A Critical Survey*. New York: Random House, 1987.

Ruether, Rosemary. *Gaia & God*: *An Ecofeminist Theology of Earth Healing*. San Francisco: Harper, 1991.

Ryokan. Trans. John Stevens, *Dewdrops on a Lotus Leaf: Zen Poems of Ryokan*. Boston: Shambhala, 1995.

Sharp, Basil. *The Adventure of Being Human*: *A Guide to Living a Fuller Life*. Washington, D.C.: Integrated Life Architects, 2000.

Smith, Huston. *The Illustrated World's Religions*: *A Guide to Our Wisdom Tradition*. San Francisco: Harper, 1994.

——. *The Religions of Man*. New York: Harper & Row, 1958.

Spong, John S. *Here I Stand*: *My Struggle for a Christianity of Integrity, Love, and Equality*. San Francisco: Harper, 2000.

——. *Why Christianity Must Change or Die*: *A Bishop Speaks to Believers in Exile*. San Francisco: Harper, 1998.

Stanfield, Brian, ed. *The Art of Focused Conversation*. Toronto: ICA Canada, 1997.

——. *The Courage to Lead*: *Transform Self, Transform Society*. Gabriola Island, Canada: New Society, 2000.

250

St. John of the Cross. *The Dark Night of the Soul & the Living Flame of Love*. San Francisco: Harper, 1995.

Swimme, Brian. *The Hidden Heart of the Cosmos: Humanity and the New Story*. Maryknoll: Orbis, 1996.

———. (with Thomas Berry) *The Universe Story*. New York: HarperCollins, 1992.

Teilhard de Chardin, Pierre. *Activation of Energy*. London: Harcourt Brace Javanovich, 1970.

———. *Building the Earth*. New York: Avon Books, 1965.

———. *Human Energy*. New York: Harcourt Brace Jovanovich, 1969.

———. *Hymn of the Universe*. New York: Harper & Row, 1961.

———. *The Future of Man*. New York: Harper & Row, 1964.

———. *The Human Phenomenon*, ed. and trans. Sarah Appleton-Weber. Brighton: Sussex Academic, 1999.

Tillich, Paul. *Biblical Religion and the Search for Ultimate Reality*. Chicago: University of Chicago, 1955.

———. *Courage to Be*. New Haven: Yale, 1952.

———. *Systematic Theology* III. Chicago: University of Chicago, 1963.

———. *The Shaking of the Foundations*. New York: Scribners, 1948.

Tutu, Desmond. *No Future Without Forgiveness*. New York: Doubleday, 1999.

Werkmeister, W. H. *Nicolai Hartmann's New Ontology*. Tallahassee: Florida State, 1990.

Wilber, Ken. *A Theory of Everything*. Shambhala, 2001.

———. *Integal Psychology*. Boston: Shambhala, 2000.

———. *One Taste: Daily Reflections on Integral Spirituality*. Boston: Shambhala, 2000.

———. *The Eye of the Spirit: An Integral Vision for a World Gone Slightly Mad*. Boston: Shambhala, 1997.

———. *The Marriage of Sense and Soul*. New York: Random House, 1998.

———. *Sex, Ecology, Spirituality: The Spirit of Evolution*. Boston: Shambhala, 1995.

Zohar, Hannah, with Ian Marshall. *SQ: Connecting with our Spiritual Intelligence*. New York: Bloomsbury, 2000.

www.ingramcontent.com/pod-product-compliance
Lightning Source LLC
La Vergne TN
LVHW011220080426
835509LV00005B/233